Jennu

Jay Haley
on
Milton H. Erickson

Jay Haley
on
Milton H. Erickson

by

Jay Haley

BRUNNER/MAZEL Publishers • New York

I gratefully acknowledge the persons and organizations who have given me the permission to reprint the papers in this book: Jeffrey K. Zeig and The Milton H. Erickson Foundation, Jossey-Bass, Inc., Brunner/Mazel, Inc., and John H. Weakland. For a complete listing of original sources and copyright data see pp. vii–viii.

Library of Congress Cataloging-in-Publication Data
Haley, Jay.
    Jay Haley on Milton H. Erickson / by Jay Haley.
        p.   cm.
    Includes bibliograhpical references.
    ISBN 0-87630-728-4
    1. Hypnotism—Therapeutic use.   2. Erickson, Milton H.
    3. Psychotherapy.   I. Title.
    RC495.H335   1993
    616.89′162—dc20   93-5375
                                                                                                            CIP

Published by
BRUNNER/MAZEL, INC.
19 Union Square West
New York, New York 10003

Manufactured in the United States of America

10 9 8 7 6 5 4 3 2 1

Contents

Acknowledgments

I wish to express my appreciation to the various sources where these papers were originally published, who have kindly given me permission to publish them here. I present them in order of publication.

"Milton H. Erickson: A Brief Biography" and the "Commentary on Milton H. Erickson, M.D." were originally published by Grune & Stratton in 1967 in a collection of articles by Dr. Erickson which I edited, *Advanced Techniques of Hypnosis and Therapy: Selected Papers of Milton H. Erickson, M.D.*, pp. 1–5 and 530–549. Copyright © 1967 by Grune & Stratton.

I am grateful to The Milton H. Erickson Foundation and to Brunner/Mazel for allowing me to republish papers from meetings of the Foundation. These include:

"Erickson's Contribution to Therapy" from *Ericksonian Approaches to Hypnosis and Psychotherapy*, pp. 5–25, edited by Jeffrey K. Zeig, Ph.D., and published by Brunner/Mazel in 1982. Copyright © 1982 by The Milton H. Erickson Foundation.

"A Review of Ordeal Therapy" from *Ericksonian Psychotherapy, Volume II: Clinical Applications*, edited by Jeffrey K. Zeig, Ph.D., and published by Brunner/Mazel in 1985 for The Milton H. Erickson Foundation, was originally published in *Ordeal Therapy: Unusual Ways to Change Behavior*, pp. 1–23, by Jay Haley, and published by Jossey-Bass in 1984. Copyright © 1984 by Jossey-Bass, Inc. It is included here with the permission of Jossey-Bass.

"Remembering Erickson: A Dialogue Between Jay Haley and John Weakland" from *Ericksonian Psychotherapy, Volume I: Structures*, pp. 585–604, edited by Jeffrey K. Zeig, Ph.D., and published by Brunner/Mazel in 1985. Copyright © 1985 by The Milton H. Erickson Foundation. It is also included here with the permission of Mr. Weakland.

"Why Not Long-Term Therapy?" from *Brief Therapy: Myths, Methods and Metaphors*, pp. 3–17, edited by Jeffrey K. Zeig, Ph.D., and Stephen G. Gilligan, Ph.D., and published by Brunner/Mazel in 1990. Copyright © 1990 by The Milton H. Erickson Foundation.

"Zen and the Art of Therapy" from *The Evolution of Psychotherapy: The Second Conference*, pp. 24–38, edited by Jeffrey K. Zeig, Ph.D., and

Introduction:
A Man Still Ahead of His Time

I met Milton H. Erickson, M.D., in San Francisco in 1953 when I attended his seminar on hypnosis. I last saw him not long before his death in 1980. Over the decades I spent many hundreds of hours with him exploring the nature of hypnosis, of human problems, and the nature of therapy. No one else influenced me more about the nature of human beings and the processes of change. During this period the field of therapy was transformed. In the 1950s Erickson was an outsider, an isolated original who was primarily known as the major medical hypnotist. His therapy approach was unusual and controversial, outside the mainstream. By the time of his death he was considered the founder of a major school of therapy, and large meetings were held in his honor. He was the mainstream of therapy, but he had not changed—the therapy stream was now running his way. What was once orthodox was vanishing, and the basic premises of therapy that he innovated were taking over the field. Instead of his admirers being heretics and at risk, they became admired themselves. Erickson's influence is even greater today—over a decade after his death.

Let me describe aspects of therapy that were orthodox in the 1950s. On each issue Erickson was proposing the opposite.

HYPNOSIS OR NOT?

Hypnosis was not taught in psychiatry and was, in fact, forbidden. Only in the late 1950s was it accepted by the American Medical Association. Erickson had used hypnosis for all of his professional life and recommended it for therapy. He was teaching weekend workshops because hypnosis was not allowed to be taught in medical school. His trainees were largely physicians and dentists since psychiatrists did not, or could not, attend without consequences. Today hypnosis is accepted and used by a large number of practitioners, and it is still to Erickson that they turn for ideas and techniques.

LONG-TERM OR SHORT-TERM?

Therapy was long-term, in fact becoming interminable. It was routine for a therapist to say to a client that he or she should not expect any change for at least a year. Often clients were told to put off life decisions, such as marriage or a change in career, during the analysis. A therapist who did brief therapy was condemned. Brief therapy was said to be shallow and merely applying a bandage to a serious problem. It helped people escape into health instead of really changing people. Clients bragged about how many years they had been in therapy. It was routine for a therapist to require the client to come several days a week.

Erickson was doing brief therapy whenever he could. He spoke of many single-session cures. He would also see someone irregularly, monthly or more, since he believed that change could occur without regular therapy sessions. Often he would correspond with a client who lived at a distance as a way of continuing the therapy. He did not consider working for a few sessions to be doing less than therapy lasting months or years (and one might note there was no outcome research that showed that long-term therapy was more effective than short-term). Today the therapy field has swung in Erickson's direction. Long-term therapy is on the defensive, and in fact disappearing. Not only have theories changed, but insurance companies are forcing therapists to learn how to do brief therapy. Erickson is still the primary source of that skill.

DIRECTIVE OR NOT

Therapists were opposed to giving any advice or a directive to a client. They interpreted or reflected back what the client was saying. By the 1950s Erickson had mastered a wide range of directives, both straightforward and indirect. He would offer advice and he would use complex directives with individuals and families. Today therapists are scrambling to learn how to give directives since the field is developing that way. Erickson is still one of the few sources of standard procedures and innovations in that area.

THE HANDLE OF THE POT

Traditionally therapists would not focus upon the problem the client offered. They would advise that the problem was only a symptom, a manifestation of something else. The deep roots of the problem were to be focused upon, not the problem itself. If asked how to relieve a symptom, the therapist would say one should not. The symptom was a manifestation of dynamics that must be worked through. Often the symptom remained after treatment, but it was said not to bother the client so much.

Erickson would focus upon the presenting problem and change the person or the family through that focus. As he once pointed out, a symptom is like the handle of a pot. If one has hold of the handle, a lot can be done with the pot. He believed clients were more cooperative if one dealt with what they were paying their money to get over. Today the therapy field is learning to focus upon the problem. Therapists are learning to explore symptoms and change them rather than seek out what is behind them, or around the corner from them. With the pressure of needing to do brief therapy, the therapist must do something about a presenting problem as quickly as possible. The time of leisurely exploration has passed. Erickson is still the primary source of how to eliminate symptoms as quickly as possible.

SHALL WE BE NEUTRAL?

Orthodox therapists were neutral. They declined to use personal influence with a client or to get personally involved. Attempting to be a blank screen that the client could project upon, they considered being personally involved a sign of psychopathology. They sat out of sight of the patient, and they spoke in a monotone while wearing a deadpan expression. In this way they tried to be of no influence on what the patient said or did. When Harry Stack Sullivan suggested that there were two people in the room on therapy, and they were both responding to each other, he was banished outside the pale.

Erickson used his personal self as much as possible to influence a client. He would persuade, cajole, joke, demand, threaten, make telephone calls, or do whatever was necessary to achieve the therapeutic goal. He argued that it was personal concern and involvement that got things done, and his diagnosis was in relation to real people in the real world, not projections. In the field today, therapists are trying to decide how much personal persuasion there should be, and they find that if one does a brief, problem-oriented therapy, one cannot be neutral and appear unconcerned.

THE PAST OR THE PRESENT?

In orthodox therapy up until the 1950s, the entire focus was on the past. It was assumed that the individual had symptoms because of past programming. The phobia was the result of a past trauma. The anxiety attack was caused by past experiences. It was assumed that symptoms were maladaptive behaviors carried over from past experiences. The present situation was largely irrelevant. Therefore, the therapy focused on the past. A wife unhappy with her husband was assumed to be projecting upon him past family experiences. The therapist would not even talk to a relative on the telephone, far less see the client and relative together.

Erickson dealt with the past, particularly by using hypnosis to relieve and change past traumas. However, he also assumed that symptoms had a present function and he would change the relationships of a client to change the problem. He was perfectly willing to see relatives, whether spouses or whole families, when he felt that would lead to a change in the client. He would involve, and develop, whatever relationships the client had.

Today therapists, particularly those who work briefly, focus upon the present situation, not the past. In fact, the phobia specialists do not even inquire about the past or search for early traumas but focus on the present. It is also assumed that a wife's anxiety can be related to her husband or to her mother and her husband. The family therapy assumption is that a symptom is adaptive to the present social situation, and that situation must be changed to change the symptom. For therapists looking for methods to change current relationships, Erickson is still a primary source.

THE GOOD AND BAD UNCONSCIOUS

Orthodox therapy considered motivation to be based upon unconscious forces. The unconscious was conceived to be an entity filled with unsavory impulses and ideas and deeply buried hostilities. The motivation of a patient was said to be his struggle to consciously control the inner hostilities striving to come out. A diagnostic interview consisted of exploring the negative aspects of the person to find out what was in the unconscious which must be relieved. The therapeutic tool was the interpretation used to bring out the unfortunate ideas and feelings of the person. All that was awful was to be remembered.

Erickson offered the view of the unconscious as a positive force. If unconscious influences were followed, the persons would benefit. He would use the example of a centipede who does well unconsciously with its 100 legs but is in trouble if it consciously tries to coordinate them. He emphasized trusting one's unconscious and following unconscious influences. As an example, if he misplaced something he would assume his unconscious did that and he would find the object at the correct time for some positive action. A diagnostic interview from this point of view explores what is in the unconscious that is positive. The client is encouraged to expand what he or she has done to solve the problem since the unconscious, if free to act, will do what is best for the person. Erickson did not make interpretations related to the unconscious. He was also willing to provide amnesia so people could forget painful experiences or remember them in a controlled, nonfrightening way.

CONCLUSION

For every issue of the orthodox therapy of his time, Erickson held an opposing view. He used hypnosis when that was not done, he did brief therapy when the only therapy was long-term, and he gave directives when nondirective therapy was the mode. He also focused on the problem when others dealt with only what was behind it, he was personally involved and not neutral, he focused upon the present more than the past, and he viewed the person as having a positive unconscious whose impulses should be encouraged. All of these positions by Erickson are becoming accepted in the field. From being an original and an outsider he has become central to the field of therapy.

Jay Haley
on
Milton H. Erickson

1

Milton H. Erickson:
A Brief Biography
(1967)

Milton H. Erickson, M.D., is generally acknowledged to be the world's leading practitioner of medical hypnosis. His writings on hypnosis are the authoritative word on techniques of inducing trance, experimental work exploring the possibilities and limits of the hypnotic experience, and investigations of the nature of the relationship between hypnotist and subject.

Perhaps less well known is the fact that Dr. Erickson has a unique approach to psychotherapy which represents a major innovation in therapeutic technique. For many years he has been developing effective and practical methods of treatment which may or may not involve the formal induction of trance. Those who think of him largely as a hypnotherapist might be surprised that he lists himself in the telephone directory as psychiatrist and family counselor.

Dr. Erickson is both a psychiatrist and a psychologist, having received his medical degree and his master's degree in psychology simultaneously. Consequently he is a Fellow of both the American Psychiatric Association and the American Psychological Association. In addition, he is a Fellow of the American Psychopathological Association, and he is an honorary member of numerous societies of medical hypnosis in Europe, Latin America, and Asia. He was the founding president of the American Society for Clinical Hypnosis as well as the founder and editor of that society's professional journal. His professional life since 1950 has included both a busy private practice in Phoenix, Arizona, and constant traveling to offer seminars in hypnosis and lectures both in the United States and many foreign countries.

Born in Aurum, Nevada, a town which has since disappeared, Dr. Erickson is one of the few people who traveled *east* in a covered wagon when his family settled on a farm in Wisconsin. His interest in hypnosis came about when he was an undergraduate student in psychology at the University of Wisconsin and observed a demonstration of hypnosis by Clark L. Hull. Impressed by what he had seen, Erickson invited Hull's subject up to his room and hypnotized him himself. From that time on he taught himself to be a hypnotist by using as subjects anyone who would hold still for him, including his fellow students, friends, and his family when he returned to his father's farm for summer vacation. In the Fall of the next year he took part in a seminar in hypnosis from Hull, which was largely devoted to examining Erickson's experiences hypnotizing people during the summer and his experimental work in the laboratory. By his third year of college, Erickson had hypnotized several hundred people, he had carried on quite a number of experiments, and he had demonstrated hypnosis for the faculty of the medical school and the psychology department as well as the staff of Mendota State Hospital.

After receiving his medical degree at the Colorado General Hospital and completing his internship and a special period of training at the Colorado Psychopathic Hospital, Erickson accepted the position of junior psychiatrist at Rhode Island State Hospital. A few months later, in April, 1930, he joined the staff of the Research Service at the Worcester State Hospital and rapidly rose from junior to senior to Chief Psychiatrist on the Research Service. Four years later, he went to Eloise, Michigan, as Director of Psychiatric Research and Training at Wayne County General Hospital and Infirmary. In addition, he became an Associate Professor of Psychiatry at the Wayne State University College of Medicine as well as a full professor in the Graduate School there. Briefly, he was concurrently a Visiting Professor of Clinical Psychology at Michigan State University in East Lansing. He did his most extensive experimentation with hypnosis at Eloise and found ideas from hypnosis particularly useful in the training of psychiatric residents.

When training psychiatrists, as well as medical students, Dr. Erickson put great emphasis upon learning how to observe a patient, and he believes that training as a hypnotist increases that ability. His own extraordinary powers of observation are legendary. Remarking that physical limitations made him more observant, he says, "I had a polio attack when 17 years old and I lay in bed without a sense of body awareness. I couldn't even tell the position of my arms or legs in bed. So I spent hours trying to locate my hand or my foot or my toes by a sense of feeling, and I became acutely aware of what movements were. Later, when I went into medicine, I learned the nature of muscles. I used that knowledge to develop an adequate use of the muscles polio had left me and to limp with the least possible strain; this took me ten years. I also became extremely aware of physical movements and this has been exceedingly useful. People use those little telltale movements, those adequate movements that are so revealing if one can notice them. So much of our communication is in our bodily movements, not in our speech. I've found that I can recognize a good piano player not by the noises he makes, but by the ways his fingers touch the keys. The sure touch, the delicate touch, the forceful touch that is so accurate. Proper playing involves such exquisite physical movement."

Dr. Erickson cannot recognize a good piano player by the noise he makes because he is tone deaf. This, too, he defines as an asset in his work. "So much is communicated by the way a person speaks," he says. "My tone deafness has forced me to pay attention to inflections in the voice. This means I'm less distracted by the content of what people say. Many patterns of behavior are reflected in the way a person says something rather than in what he says."

Dr. Erickson is also color blind, and this too became an asset when he experimented with producing color blindness with hypnosis. Experimenter bias was avoided. To this writer, one of the more extraordinary scenes in research is reported in "The Hypnotic Induction of Hallucinatory Color Vision Followed by Pseudo Negative After-Images." Experimental subjects in trance were shown white sheets of paper and they hallucinated colors upon them. Then they were immediately shown white sheets of paper and hallucinated the after-image, this being the complementary color. Holding up the white sheets was Dr. Erickson, who could not visualize the colors whether awake or in trance. (The one color he can enjoy is purple. Although it might not always be an appropriate color, he manages to surround himself with it whenever he can. He wears purple ties and sport shirts, his pajamas are purple, and the bathroom in his house has purple walls.)

Dr. Erickson likes to describe therapy as a way of helping patients extend their limits, and he has spent his own life doing that. In 1919 when he was stricken with polio, he was informed that he would never again be able to walk. After spending many hours concentrating on achieving a flicker of movement in the muscles of his legs, he was up on crutches within a year. He even managed to obtain and hold a sitting-down job in a cannery to help finance his way into the University of Wisconsin. After his first year at the university, he was advised by his physician to spend his summer vacation getting a great deal of exercise in the sunshine without using his legs. Deciding that a canoe trip would provide the appropriate exercise, Erickson set out in June in a 17-foot canoe, wearing a bathing suit, a pair of overalls, and a knotted handkerehief on his head for a hat. He did not have the strength in his legs to pull his canoe out of the water and he could swim only a few feet. His supplies for his summer's voyage consisted of a small sack of beans, another of rice, and a few cooking utensils. His wealth for the purchase of more supplies consisted of $2.32. With these provisions, he spent from June until September traveling through the lakes of Madison, down the Yahara River, down the Rock River, into the Mississippi and on down to a few miles above St. Louis, then back up the Illinois River, through the Hennepin Canal to the Rock River, and so to Madison. He foraged for his food along the way by eating what fish he could catch, finding edible plants on the river banks when he camped at night, and harvesting crops from the Mississippi. These crops consisted of the bushels of peelings the cooks on the river steamers threw overboard. Among them, there were always a few whole potatoes or apples thrown out by mistake. By the end of the summer, he had traveled a distance of 1,200 miles with almost no supplies or money, without sufficient strength in his legs to carry his canoe over the dams which blocked his way, and so physically weak when he began that he could hardly paddle a few miles downstream without getting overtired.

The journey was even more complicated for Erickson than it would have been for anyone else. He was the kind of young man who refused to ask assistance of anyone. That is, he refused to ask directly, but he enjoyed arranging the situation so that people would "spontaneously" do things for him. In telling about his canoe trip, he said, "I would paddle within hailing distance of a fishing boat. Since I tanned very deeply and wore that knotted handkerchief on my head, the fishermen would get curious and hail me to ask a few questions. I would tell them I was a pre-med student at the University of Wisconsin canoeing for my health. They would ask how the fishing was, I would reply that the day was yet young. Invariably they gave me fish at the end of the conversation, though I never asked for any. Usually they tried to give me catfish, but I always refused them. Catfish were much too expensive and they were making their living fishing. When I refused the catfish they would give me double or three times the amount of Mississippi perch."

Although he could not carry his canoe over a dam, Dr. Erickson would never ask for assistance. He says, "I would shinny up one of the poles that are always around dams. Soon people would gather and look up curiously at me sitting up there reading a German book I brought with me in preparation for my medical studies. Finally someone would ask me what on earth I was doing up on that pole. I would look up from my book and say that I was waiting to get my canoe carried over the dam. This always meant volunteer service."

With an occasional day's work along the river, and volunteer service, Erickson completed his summer of canoeing, extending his limits by putting himself in good physical shape. When he returned, his chest measurement had increased six inches, he could swim a mile, and he could paddle upstream against a four-mile current from dawn to dusk. He could also carry his own canoe over a dam.

Years later, in 1952, Dr. Erickson suffered a rare medical occurrence when he was stricken with another strain of polio. This attack markedly affected his right arm and side. Within a year he had made one of the more difficult hikes in the mountains of Arizona with the use of two canes.

Dr. Erickson left Eloise and settled in Phoenix, largely for his health. His private practice is conducted in a unique setting. The office in which he sees patients is in his home, a small three-bedroom brick house in a pleasant neighborhood. His waiting room is the living room, and his patients have been exposed over the years to his family life and his eight children. He sees patients in an office which is just large enough to contain his desk, a few chairs, and bookcases. On the wall is a picture of his parents who lived until into their nineties, and scattered about are family mementos from over the years, including a stuffed badger. This office is almost absurdly unpretentious for a psychiatrist of Dr. Erickson's stature, but his attitude toward it is that it is convenient. A young disciple who was setting up a practice in Phoenix was seeking a proper office, and he once protested to Dr. Erickson that his office was not all that it might be. Dr. Erickson replied that it had been even less fancy when he first began practice, since the room had in it only a card table and two chairs. "However," he said, "*I* was there."

Besides his private practice, Dr. Erickson carries on many of his professional activities from his home, including editing *The American Journal of Clinical Hypnosis* with the assistance of his wife. Elizabeth Erickson has worked with her husband in many activities over the years and co-authored a number of papers with him. They met when she was a psychology student and laboratory assistant at Wayne State University, and were married in 1936. Dr. Erickson, who had been previously married, brought three children to the marriage. Since then, they have had five more children, with a consequently lively family life. Mrs. Erickson once estimated that they would have at least one teenager in the family for 30 consecutive years. The last two are now in their teens, and the earlier children are married and bringing home grandchildren.

Dr. Erickson uses examples from his life with his children when discussing hypnosis and therapy. Readers who might wonder what it is like to have a father who is a master hypnotist could enjoy the article "Pediatric Hypnotherapy." Dr. Erickson describes handling an incident with his son Robert to illustrate how to deal with children in pain. Robert fell down the back stairs, split his lip, and knocked his upper tooth back into the maxilla. He was bleeding and screaming with pain and fright. His parents rushed to him and saw that it was an emergency. Dr. Erickson writes,

No effort was made to pick him up. Instead, as he paused for breath for fresh screaming, he was told quickly, simply, sympathetically, and emphatically, "That hurts awful, Robert. That hurts terrible."

Right then, without any doubt, my son knew that I knew what I was talking about. He could agree with me and he knew I was agreeing with him completely. Therefore he could listen respectfully to me, because I had demonstrated that I understood the situation fully.

Rather than reassure the boy, Dr. Erickson proceeded in typical fashion:

Then I told Robert, "And it will keep right on hurting." In this simple statement, I named his own fear, confirmed his own judgment of the situation, demonstrated my good intelligent grasp of the entire matter and my entire agreement with him, since right then he could foresee a lifetime of anguish and pain for himself.

The next step for him and for me was to declare, as he took another breath, "And you really wish it would stop hurting." Again, we were in full agreement and he was gratified and even encouraged in his wish. And it was *his* wish, deriving entirely from within him and constituting his own urgent need.

With the situation so defined, I could then offer a suggestion with some certainty of his acceptance. This suggestion was, "Maybe it will stop hurting in a little while, in just a minute or two."

This was a suggestion in full accord with his own needs and wishes and, because it was qualified by "maybe it will," it was not in contradiction to his own understandings of the situation. Thus he could accept the idea and initiate his response to it.

Dr. Erickson then shifted to another important matter. As he puts it:

Robert knew that he hurt, that he was a damaged person; he could see his blood upon the pavement, taste it in his mouth and see it on his hands. And yet, like all other human beings, he too could desire narcissistic distinction in his misfortune, along with the desire for even more narcissistic comfort. Nobody wants a picayune headache; since a headache must be endured, let it be so colossal that only the sufferer could endure it. Human pride is so curiously good and comforting! Therefore, Robert's attention was doubly directed to two vital issues of comprehensible importance to him by the simple statements, "That's an awful lot of blood on the pavement. Is it good, red, strong blood? Look carefully, Mother, and see. I think it is, but I want you to be sure."

Examination proved it to be good strong blood, but it was necessary to verify this by examination of it against the white background of the bathroom sink. In this way the boy, who had ceased crying in pain and fright, was cleaned up. When he went to the doctor for stitches the question was whether he would get as many as his sister had once been given. The suturing was done without anesthetic on a boy who was an interested participant in the procedure.

Although Dr. Erickson has a local practice, many of the patients who come to see him have traveled considerable distances. Patients will fly from as far as New York or from Mexico City to be relieved of their troubles almost as if visiting a surgeon, and others commute irregularly from the West Coast. In recent years both his practice and his teaching have been curtailed because of illness. When he attends an occasional meeting now it is in a wheelchair, and his work load at home is reduced.

Many of the admirers of Dr. Erickson have felt that his approach to therapy and hypnosis have not been adequately presented to the psychiatric community. Although he is well known and a figure of some controversy, his basic writings have not been easily available. He has published over 100 papers on a variety of subjects over the years, but the reader of an occasional article or the student at a lecture cannot properly appreciate the magnitude of this man's work or the innovations he has introduced.

2

Commentary on
Milton H. Erickson, M.D.
(1967)

In every profession, there is an occasional man who can be called an "original" because he works within a profession while deviating markedly from the ways of most of his colleagues. Sometimes such a man persuades the profession to follow him, and at other times he remains an outsider and does not make a ripple in the stream. Sigmund Freud took a unique direction and offered both a set of powerful ideas and an organization to foster and perpetuate a following. Harry Stack Sullivan did not organize, but the force of his new ideas and his personal influence as a teacher impressed his views upon the profession. As an innovator in psychiatry, Milton H. Erickson can be classed with Freud and Sullivan. Whether he will have as great an influence on the field is yet to be determined.

Like Freud, Erickson's major ideas came out of the field of hypnosis. Unlike Freud, he has stayed within the hypnotic tradition and reached quite different conclusions about the nature of psychopathology and therapeutic change. Like Sullivan, Erickson has placed greater emphasis upon the relationship than upon the individual. Unlike both Freud and Sullivan, Erickson's primary interest has been the exploration of diverse techniques for producing therapeutic change. What is most original about him, and what makes his approach not a simple school or method, is his flexibility; he is willing to orient his therapeutic approach to the particular problem before him. In a period of psychiatric history where a man was judged by whether or not he followed the proper theory and method, Erickson originated experimental therapy.

In the first half of this century, during the period of Erickson's development, there was a trend toward defense against innovation in the psychiatric profession. As psychoanalysis gained prestige in the consulting room and the university, there was a shift from the original exploratory approach of Freud to a ritualized treatment method and the repetition of stereotyped ideas. In this process, a peculiar change in emphasis took place in psychiatry. Complex human dilemmas were forced into a narrow theoretical scheme, and therapy began to be judged by whether the proper procedures were followed and not by whether results were obtained. It was in this climate that Erickson developed a wide variety of therapeutic techniques and tenaciously pursued the idea that the type of treatment should vary with the nature of the patient's problem. In the last decade, the idea of exploring new methods has been adopted by many psychiatrists and has led to such innovations as behavior therapy, conditioning treatment, and marital and family therapy. We have seen the passing of an emphasis upon ritual and a move toward judging therapeutic procedures by results instead of conformity to a particular school. It has even become respectable now to work in different ways with different types of patients.

Examining his writings, one can see that Erickson has carried the idea of experimentation throughout his professional work. It is as if he said to himself, "If I do this, what will that person do, and would another person respond differently?" In that sense, he has devoted his life to exploring the nature of one person's influence over another. With experimental investigations of hypnosis, he tested the limits of interpersonal influence over a person's sensory apparatus and behavior. He examined such questions as whether he could influence a person to be unable to hear, unable to see, unable to see colors, unable to experience physical sensations, unable to resist anti-social influences, and unable to be aware of the thought processes behind his behavior. Conversely, he examined how much could be achieved in the increase of sensation and perception. He explored the limits of unconscious mentation as well as the possible changes in a person's subjective perception of time and space.

The series of research papers reporting these experimental investigations represent some of the most solid work ever done in the field. Replication of many of the studies would require an investigator approaching subjects with the same care. Erickson routinely spent several hours inducing a trance before an experiment was attempted, and he took into account the individual idiosyncracies of each subject as well as an extraordinary number of other variables which might influence the experimental outcome. He assumed that the possibility of experimenter bias was part of the peril of such investigations, and his precautions to insure that a subject's response was genuine and not simulated were elaborate. Perhaps most important, he recognized the laboratory setting as a variable which can set limits upon the nature and validity of findings and was willing to conduct some of his investigations in the social arena. When today many hypnotic experiments are done with brief, standardized inductions in an atmosphere of spurious objectivity, Erickson's work, in contrast, appears an art as well as a science.

In the field of psychotherapy, Erickson has applied an experimental approach to both the investigation of psychiatric problems and to ways of resolving them. When it was assumed that the words and behavior of a patient were a produet of certain types of unconscious mentation, he tested this notion by "programming" specific ideas into a subject and then he observed the outcome behavior. As reported in "Experimential Demonstrations of the Psychopathology of Everyday Life," he provided experimental subjects with ideas and emotions, rendered these amnesic, and observed the overt behavior which followed. This work included the implantation of "complexes" in the form of false memories of past traumas to determine their effects on behavior. One of the better analyses of human communication extant is in his paper "The Method Employed to Formulate a Complex Story for the Induction of an Experimental Neurosis." Erickson's detailed analysis of why he used each word in the story of the past incident shows an extraordinary awareness of the intricacies of interpersonal involvement. His concern with the most subtle details of behavior is evident throughout his papers, particularly in such reports as "The Permanent Relief of an Obsessional Phobia Through Communication with an Unsuspected Dual Personality" (written with L. S. Kubie).

Whether doing research or therapy, the procedures used by Erickson will vary with the needs of a particular person, a situation, a time, and his own needs. His therapeutic approach is characterized by the view that human problems are infinitely diverse, while his therapeutic stance appears infinitely flexible. Yet there is a consistency in the ways he deals with patients which gives his treatment a recognizable style.

Part of the problem when examining Erickson's therapeutic technique is the fact that there is no adequate theoretical framework available for describing it. His operations are based upon a new set of premises about the nature of psychopathology and therapeutic change, and these premises have not been systematically stated. Writing about his cases, Erickson tends to describe them within a theoretical framework of hypnosis, or of conditioning, or of psychodynamic theory. When one examines what he actually does with a patient, these traditional views do not seem appropriate. Out of a study of his work can come a new perspective in the field of therapy, but only if one is willing to examine what he does with a fresh view. From the traditional way of thinking, what Erickson does is often not reasonable; from the view of his approach, what is usually done in traditional therapy is often not reasonable.

When Erickson describes a case, he presents what the patient did and what he did, forcing us to examine the behavior of both participants in the interchange. It is this artifact of his case presentations which makes him appear more manipulative than other therapists, as well as his willingness to concede that therapy is an art of manipulation. Yet when one speaks privately to therapists of any school and asks them to describe what they actually did with a patient, they too appear manipulative. One learns that many of the kinds of operations done by Erickson are done by good therapists. Some psychiatrists wouldn't require a married couple who both wet the bed to conjointly wet the bed, as reported in "Indirect Hypnotic Therapy of an Enuretic Couple," but skilled therapists will actively intervene into patients' lives and require different types of behavior from them. However, in their case reports such therapists often will not mention these activities but will describe what should have been done according to the theory of a particular school rather than what was actually done.

The information about what Erickson does in therapy is of several kinds; his papers, which include case reports and discussion, his demonstrations of how he works with a patient before a group, and his lectures and conversations about therapy. Many of his lectures, demonstrations, and conversations have been tape-recorded; Erickson is probably the most recorded therapist in history, and plans for a depository of such recordings are being made. The best information on the way Erickson works is in his case descriptions. However, many of his therapeutic procedures have not yet been written up and one can learn about them only from conversations with him. One also learns that although the "facts" of a particular case remain the same in his written and conversational reports, there are always more aspects of the case which are not mentioned in any particular context. He tends to emphasize those aspects most pertinent to the person with whom he is conversing. The reader of his case reports must keep in mind that Erickson is attempting to communicate with an audience trained in more traditional views, and he tends to adapt what he says to that audience.

I will attempt some generalizations about the practical and theoretical aspects of Erickson's operations with information drawn from his published writings and from many hours of recorded conversations with him.[1] The view of his work offered here might or might not agree with Erickson's own views. His description of his work is available in his papers and what is said here is an adjunct to, and a commentary on, those writings. The reader can examine his papers and perhaps conceive of his work in a different way. Some of the more practical aspects of his therapy can be described first.

Most therapists, and therapeutic approaches, tend to be restricted to a type of patient, but Erickson's cases cover the full range of human problems. He has eased the strains of birth at the beginning of the human career, and he has helped ease the human being gracefully out of this world by treating terminal cancer patients (as in "Hypnosis in Painful Terminal Illness"). His case studies include all of life's stages; child problems, adolescent difficulties, marital problems, and the dilemmas of middle age and retirement. Not only has he worked with the neurotic as well as the psychotic, but he has been willing to treat the less clearly psychiatric problems of the brain damaged and physically handicapped (as in "Hypnotically Oriented Psychotherapy in Organic Disease.")

For Erickson, the possible unit of treatment is not only the individual; it will also be the marital couple or the total family group. He might work with a symptom as an individual problem or as a product of a type of marriage. When focusing upon the married couple, he likes to establish his freedom to work with them either together in the session or separately. With child problems, he might exclude the parents in one case and require their participation in another. He has even been known to have a family session with only the patient present by having the patient in trance hallucinate the other family members in the room.

---

1. Research on Dr. Erickson's work was a part of Gregory Bateson's project for the study of communication. Many of the conversations with Erickson were conducted with John Weakland as part of a joint exploration of hypnosis and this approach to therapy.

Although he largely works in his office, Erickson will venture out into the community whenever the treatment requires it. He seems as comfortable in the patient's home or place of business, or an airport waiting room, as he does in his own office. Since he often does therapy without calling it therapy, he will work on a person's problems while ostensibly giving only a demonstration of hypnosis before a large group or while carrying on a social conversation. When necessary, he will accompany the patient to the problem situation; for example, when a young man fainted each time he attempted to enter a particular restaurant, Erickson took him there to dinner in such a way that the problem was eliminated. He has even raced a small patient, a little girl, down the street on a bicycle.

The therapeutic hour is rigidly set by many therapists and time is often considered a fixed entity. To Erickson, time is malleable. With some patients, he will work the 50-minute hour, others he will see for a few minutes, and some patients will be seen in sessions extending over several hours. He is flexible in his scheduling of patients and may see them daily, weekly, or quite irregularly. He will also influence the patient's sense of time with time distortion techniques, he will disorient the patient in time with confusion techniques, and he can eliminate time altogether with amnesia for various experiences.

The duration of his treatment will vary from long-term commitments to remarkably brief therapy. Patients will travel considerable distances to see him for a day or a week, much as they might visit a surgeon. He will have regularly spaced appointments with some patients, but with others, he might see them a few hours spaced over many months. It is not uncommon for him to have therapeutic sessions after giving a lecture or seminar, and he has been known to treat by telephone and continue treatment by correspondence.

Just as he will play with time, Erickson will also make therapeutic use of fees paid by patients. He usually requires a set fee, but some patients will be required to set the fee and keep track of it. Others will not be charged an hourly fee but one contingent upon results.

THE TREATMENT APPROACH

Just as Erickson will vary the practical aspects of his therapy, such as the place, time, and fee, so does the kind of involvement he has with a patient vary with the patient. Although he will repeat many of the same treatment procedures on similar patients, as anyone with a busy practice must, his approach assumes that what he does must be different with each patient. Carl Whitaker once said that he most enjoyed a treatment session when he could say afterwards, "I never did that before." Erickson expresses a similar pleasure, but it does not seem to come from his desire to be spontaneous in his therapy as much as it does from his endless curiosity about what would happen if he tried something different. When the *n*th case of psychogenic headache or phobia comes in the door, he can use any one of several procedures which have worked well in the past. Yet he seems to prefer a variation which fits his own interests at that time and the needs of this particular patient. It is this variety which makes his therapeutic approach difficult to encapsulate in some general theory of therapy. Obviously, there are basic principles on which he operates; one can recognize an Erickson therapeutic procedure as easily as a Picasso painting. Yet to find the regularities in his various procedures and present them in a systematic way requires an oversimplification which does considerable violence to the subtleties of his technique. It is like pointing out that Picasso's paintings are made up of bold colors and quite a few angular lines. However, I will attempt a few generalizations here, as I have elsewhere,[2] to point up some of the factors his different therapeutic approaches seem to have in common. Although these factors are presented as separate entities, they fit together into a coherent treatment approach.

The Therapeutic Posture

To deal with the varieties of human dilemmas, a therapist must be capable of a wide range of behavior with patients. Don D. Jackson once in conversation characterized one of his major goals in therapy as maximizing his own freedom to maneuver with patients; this theme is apparent throughout Erickson's work. With one patient he might do no more than sit and listen, while with another he offers practical advice and with another he will use complex and subtle directives. He does not mind being severe with a patient and requiring an ordeal, nor does he mind being kind. If he draws a line, it is against offering the usual kinds of

---

2. *Strategies of Psychotherapy,* Grune & Stratton, 1963.

reassurance or offering pity to a person in distress; he does not consider that humane or helpful. He can also cheerfully work with patients who like him or those who dislike him.

Erickson believes therapists should not limit their approaches because of loyalty to a method or a teacher. He once described this view in a lecture on hypnotic and therapeutic technique: "One of the important things to remember about technique," he said, "is your willingness to learn this technique and that technique and then to recognize that you, as an individual personality, are quite different from any of your teachers who taught you a particular technique. You need to extract from the various techniques the particular elements that allow you to express yourself as a personality. The next most important thing about a technique is your awareness of the fact that every patient who comes in to you represents a different personality, a different attitude, a different background of experience. Your approach to him must be in terms of him as a person with a particular frame of reference for that day and the immediate situation. Bear in mind that it is the patient who is the important element in the entire physician-patient relationship and be willing to avoid following any *one* teaching or any *one* technique; express your own personality only to the extent that it is requisite to meet the patient and get that patient to respond to you. Then you need to use the technique, the approach, the manner, the understanding that will enable the patient to orient to what is going to happen.

"I dislike authoritative techniques and much prefer the permissive techniques as a result of my own experience. What your patient does and what he learns must be learned from within himself. There is not anything you can force into that patient. There is little opportunity with the authoritarian technique for the patient to take on the things that you start and then develop them further in the way that meets his needs. But there are times when the patient comes to you because he wants you to take responsibility, and there are times when you should take on such a responsibility, so you need to be aware of authoritative techniques and be willing to use them. However, it ought to be your authoritative technique, not that of someone else.

"You must also recognize that understanding authority is an individual matter. There are some patients who cannot understand unless you take a figurative baseball bat and hit them over the head with it, and if this is the case you ought to do it. But I think you have the privilege of deciding whether the bat shall be of soft wood or of hard wood. Yours is the privilege of defining what kind of a bat you use, and then you use it so that your patient abides by your definition. You can tell a patient, 'Shut up and sit down right now!' That is one kind of a hard wood bat. But you can also say: 'I don't know just exactly when you are going to sit down, but suppose you try to hold that chair down on the floor right now.' You have said the same thing with a soft wood bat and the patient knows it. The patient is grateful to you because that is the kind of a patient he is and because you have used tactfulness or a sort of flippant attitude in manifesting your authority.

"Remember that whatever way you choose to work must be your own way, because you cannot really imitate someone else. In dealing with the crucial situations of therapy, you must express yourself adequately, not as an imitation."

Expectation of Change

It might be assumed that a therapist in the business of changing people would expect them to change, but this is not always so. Underlying the approach of many therapists is a pessimism about the possibility of real change in the life style of a patient. This view might be partly derived from the traditional idea that psychiatric problems are determined from an early age and change is slow and difficult.

Erickson appears to approach each patient with an expectation that change is not only possible but inevitable. There is a sureness which exudes from him, although he can be unsure if he wishes, and an attitude of confidence as if it would surprise him if change did not occur. His positive view is not necessarily affected by the length of time a patient has had a problem or the amount of therapy previously experienced. In fact, he likes the challenge of patients who have failed in previous therapy. Approaching each situation as a new one, he is willing to assume some changes in life must occur slowly, but he also accepts the idea that lifelong habits can sometimes change overnight. Characteristically, he acts as if change for the better is a natural development.

Emphasis on the Positive

To Erickson, normal behavior and growth is the process of living and psychopathology an interference with that process. Within the individual, the positive forces are striving to take over, and his therapeutic focus is upon letting that happen. This view arises from his conception of the unconscious, which is in sharp contrast to the Freudian view that the unconscious is a morass of conflicting drives and unsavory types of ideas. To Erickson, the unconscious is a positive force which will arrange what is best for the individual if he stops interfering with it. An analogy he uses is that of walking; to begin to walk consciously is to stumble, while to leave walking to the unconscious means easy locomotion. This view grows out of the emphasis on the positive nature of the unconscious in traditional hypnosis. However, a distinction should be made between what Erickson might say to a patient about the patient's unconscious and what he says about the nature of the unconscious when analyzing that concept.

As a consequence of his positive view, Erickson does not explore the unfortunate thoughts or desires of a patient in any way that indicates there are even worse thoughts and desires outside the patient's awareness. Instead, out of a conversational exploration will come an appreciation of the positive aspects of the patient's thoughts. The same approach is carried by Erickson into marital and family work. He does not focus upon helping a married couple find out how hostile they feel about each other, but he will let them discover the better aspects of their relationship.

Typically what the patient defines as a defect or a sign of an unsavory character will be redefined by Erickson. The large nose on a female becomes that which gives her individuality, and the gap between the teeth of a young lady provides her the opportunity to squirt water playfully at a young man. A major skill of Erickson is the way he enforces a positive view without it appearing mere compensation or reassurance. To Erickson, the positive view is the realistic one.

Emphasis on Accepting What the Patient Offers

The most paradoxical aspect of Erickson's therapy is his willingness to accept what the patient offers while simultaneously inducing a change. Therapy is a process of accepting the patient's way while simultaneously diverting the patient in new directions. It is like diverting a stream of water so that the stream's own force is used to cut a new pathway. For example,

in "An Hypnotic Technique for Resistant Patients" he describes his way
of dealing with the openly hostile patient:

> There are many types of difficult patients who seek psychotherapy
> and yet are openly hostile, antagonistic, resistant, defensive, and
> present every appearance of being unwilling to accept the therapy
> they have come to seek. . . . Such resistance should be openly
> accepted, in fact, graciously accepted, since it is a vitally important
> communication of a part of their problems and often can be used
> as an opening into their defenses. This is something that the patient
> does not realize; rather, he may be distressed emotionally since he
> often interprets his behavior as uncontrollable, unpleasant, and
> uncooperative rather than as an informative exposition of his
> important needs. The therapist who is aware of this, particularly if
> well skilled in hypnotherapy, can easily and often quickly transform
> these often seemingly uncooperative forms of behavior into a good
> rapport, a feeling of being understood, and an attitude of hopeful
> expectancy of successfully achieving the goals being sought. . . .
> Perhaps this can be illustrated by the somewhat extreme example
> of a new patient whose opening statement as he entered the office
> characterized all psychiatrists as being best described by a commonly
> used profane vulgarity. The immediate reply was made, "You un-
> doubtedly have a damn good reason for saying *that and even more.*"
> The italicized words were not recognized by the patient as a direct
> intentional suggestion to be more communicative, but they were
> most effective.

In a similar way he will accept the behavior of the patient who is not
openly hostile but frightened. He reports:[3]

> Ann, 21, entered the office hesitantly, fearfully. She had been hesi-
> tant and fearful over the telephone. She expressed an absolute cer-
> tainty over the telephone that I would not like to see her. Accordingly,
> she was urged to come. As she entered the office she said, "I told you
> so. I will go now. My father is dead, my mother is dead, my sister
> is dead, and that is all that's left for me." She was urged to take a seat,

---

and after some rapid thinking I realized that the only possible understanding this girl had of intercommunication was that of unkindness
and brutality. Hence, brutality would be used to convince her of
sincerity. Any other possible approach, any kindness, would be mis-
interpreted. She could not possibly believe courteous language . . .

Her history was briefly taken. Then she was asked the two important questions. "How tall are you and how much do you weigh?"
With a look of extreme emotional distress, she answered, "I am 4
feet 10 inches. I weigh between 250 and 260 pounds. I am just a
plain, fat slob. Nobody would ever look at me except with disgust."
This offered a suitable opening. She was told, "You haven't really told
the truth. I am going to say this simply so that you will know about
yourself and understand that I know about you. Then you will
believe, really believe, what I have to say to you. You are *not* a plain,
fat, disgusting slob. You are the fattest, homeliest, most disgustingly
horrible bucket of lard I have ever seen and it is appalling to have
to look at you." (Only after six months of this "accepting" did Erickson
let the girl reduce and become attractive enough to marry.)

It isn't only in his opening maneuvers that Erickson accepts the needs
of his patients. The general treatment of a case has this focus. The
"acceptance" usually takes the form of accepting a framework but defining
it in such a way that change can occur. One can choose an example almost
at random from his case studies, but a rather bizarre case reported in
"Special Techniques of Brief Hypnotherapy" can be used for illustration.
A young man who wished to be drafted had the problem of being unable
to urinate unless he did so through an 8- or 10-inch wooden or iron tube.
Erickson accepted this need and persuaded the young man to use a
somewhat longer bamboo tube. After this agreement that the length and
material could be changed, the young man was led to discover that his
fingers around his penis also made an adequate tube, and finally he was
pleased to accept the idea that his penis was in itself an adequate tube.

Erickson puts particular emphasis upon symptoms as being the way
the patient communicates with the therapist, and this way of communicating must be accepted. If a patient announces that her headaches are
a necessity, Erickson will agree with her, but there is then the question
of length of headache and frequency and perhaps once a year will do. At
times, Erickson's acceptance can be seen as a part of his "contract" with

the patient. I recall a farm worker who came to him and defined himself as a dumb moron. Erickson accepted this label but led the patient to accept the idea that even a dumb moron could learn to typewrite to exercise his fingers, read to improve his home cooking, and even go to college to find out how many courses he would fail. Only after the patient was successful in college did Erickson drop the agreement that he was a dumb moron.

This process of "accepting" would seem to come directly from hypnotic technique where a subject's resistances are not opposed but encouraged. If a subject is asked to have a hand feel light and reports it is getting heavy, the hypnotist says that is fine and it can get heavier yet. Such a response accepts the relationship and defines the resistant behavior as a cooperative change in sensation. Erickson's therapeutic procedures follow in this tradition of accepting and encouraging the patient's offerings. However, accepting a patient's idea that he must be miserable does not necessarily mean that one is reinforcing his need to be miserable as a naive view of conditioning theory might indicate. The acceptance can later be followed by a move for a change, and the change is more likely to happen if the need for misery is first accepted.

Emphasis on the Range of Possibilities

Erickson not only accepts a range of possible therapeutic approaches for himself, but he assumes a range of alternative ways of behaving for the patient. Patients often conceive of their situation as a trap in which there is only one possible solution and this an unfortunate one. Erickson sees life as infinitely various. There are a multiplicity of career choices, a vast variety of ways of dealing with one's intimates, and an infinite number of ways of looking at a single situation. Facing the restricted view of a patient, Erickson might ease a different variation into it, or he might shatter that way of thinking and let the patient discover the multitude of other possible views. His ability to re-label as positive those aspects of life the patient sees as negative is one of the ways he alters the patient's view. He will also use a variety of jokes, puns, and puzzles with patients who have a particularly rigid set. When a patient insists he is absolutely right and knows what is so, Erickson will give him the task of putting 12 trees in 6 rows containing 4 each. When the patient is convinced the task is impossible, Erickson will show him how easily it can be done.

Willingness to Take Responsibility

The question of responsibility is a crucial one in therapy. Some therapists argue that the patient should take full responsibility for his life decisions and the therapist should not influence him in any way about these decisions. However, anyone well trained in hypnosis is sufficiently aware of interpersonal influence to know that a therapist cannot *not* influence the life decisions of a patient. It is not a question whether one should take the responsibility of influencing important decisions of a patient, but how one should label where the responsibility resides.

Erickson assumes he is going to influence a patient's life whatever he does, even if he tries not to, and the question is both how to do it effectively and how to label what is happening. If a patient asks for direction, many therapists will only turn the responsibility back upon him. Erickson is willing to operate in that way with some patients, but he is also quite willing to take full responsibility for a decision if he feels it is necessary. He will intervene into a patient's life by requiring a change of job, a change of residence, or a new type of behavior. He is also willing to say to a patient having difficulty with his parents, "You leave your parents to me." At the same time, however, Erickson puts great emphasis upon therapy as a procedure where it is agreed that the patient is to take responsibility for his own life.

While willing to take charge and direct a patient, Erickson is also willing to go to the other extreme and put the entire responsibility for change upon the patient, even letting the patient decide what is to be done in the therapy and how (cf. "The Burden of Responsibility in Effective Psychotherapy.") As in all issues of this kind, Erickson assumes that the question of how much responsibility the therapist should acknowledge depends upon the particular patient before him and not upon a general rule.

Blocking Off Symptomatic Behavior

Erickson approaches symptomatic behavior as a type of malfunctioning. His concern is not with the supposed "roots" of the symptom in the ideation of the patient but with its current function in the patient's situation. The therapeutic goal is to change the symptomatic behavior into behavior which is more functional in the developing life of the patient. He approaches the symptom directly and does not discuss with the patient what is "behind" the symptom. In some cases, he may ease a patient into a different style of behaving, while with others he will block off the symptomatic behavior so that it cannot persist. He may do this by re-labeling the behavior, by taking it over and changing it under direction, or by providing an ordeal which makes it impossible for the patient to continue with symptomatic behavior. If the patient who is ashamed and guilty of a wet bed can become temporarily ashamed and guilty for having a dry bed, as reported in "Special Techniques of Brief Hypnotherapy," he is being eased out of his symptom. Similarly, if a young man who wets the bed must get up in the middle of the night, take a mile walk, and climb back into that wet bed, then he reaches a point where he must give up wetting the bed. Typically, Erickson arranges ordeals for patients which are useful, such as providing needed exercise. The patient is thereby forced to improve himself since, as long as he continues the ordeal, that is good for him, and if he abandons it because the symptom is gone, that is good for him too.

Therapists who have never worked with direct relief of symptoms have perpetuated the belief that if a patient recovers from one he will develop something worse. This has not been so in Erickson's experience or others who work with similar methods. Usually when a person changes symptomatic behavior in one area, he also recovers from distress in other areas. At times, Erickson may offer an alternative for the symptom; more often, he seems to take it for granted that if the patient is dealt with properly, more positive functioning occurs when malfunctioning behavior is eliminated.

Change Occurs in Relation to the Therapist

Although Erickson has great respect for the force of ideas in changing a person's life, he assumes that an idea most effectively brings about change in a particular kind of relationship. One of his goals in working with patients is to establish an intense relationship; one in which what he says and does is of crucial importance to the patient. He does not think that the intensity of this relationship just happens, as in a "spontaneous" transference relationship, but that it is a product of the way he deliberately deals with the patient and the patient deals with him. Within the frame-work of an intense relationship, he will bring about change by arranging cooperation with him or rebellion against him. Sometimes, he suggests ways the patient should behave and the patient cooperates and finds himself changing. At other times, Erickson will persuade the patient to make a necessary change by rebelling against him. For example, he reports the way he motivated a patient in "Hypnotically Oriented Psychotherapy in Organic Disease."

> The plan devised was complex and involved; sometimes it varied not only from day to day but within the day itself so that, outside of certain items, the patient never knew what to expect, and even what was done often did not seem to make much sense to her. As a result, the patient was kept in a striving, seeking, frustrated struggling and emotional state in which anger, bewilderment, disgust, impatience and an intense, almost burning desire, to take charge and do things in an orderly and sensible manner became overwhelming. (During the writing of the paper, the patient was interested in what was being included and pointed out that many times, "I hated you horribly, you made me so furious and the madder I got, the more I tried.")[4]

Often Erickson will report cases in which a patient recovered to prove him wrong. For example, in "Special Techniques of Brief Hypnotherapy" he reports a case of a bride who panicked when faced with consummating her marriage. Erickson gave her an instruction which involved setting the range of days when sexual relations could occur and Erickson expressed a particular preference for Friday. As he puts it, "This listing of all the days of the week with emphasis about the writer's preference for Friday was systematically repeated until she began to show marked annoyance." The following Friday the woman's husband reported, "She told me to tell you what happened last night. It happened so quick I never had a chance. She practically raped me. And she woke me up before midnight to do it again. Then this morning she was laughing and when I asked her why, she told me to tell you that it wasn't Friday. I told her that today was Friday and she just laughed and said you would understand that it wasn't Friday."

---

4. This example also illustrates that Dr. Erickson often has his patients read papers reporting their cases to insure accuracy.

As in many of his cases treated in this way, Erickson likes to report, "The subsequent outcome was a continued happy marital adjustment, the purchase of a home, and the birth of three wanted children at two-year intervals."

At times, Erickson will sharply focus resistance to him on one area in such a way that a patient follows a directive to prove him wrong. For example, in "The Identification of a Secure Reality," he wished to persuade a helpless mother to literally sit upon her troublemaking son for a period of hours. He reports that she had various objections to this procedure; however, she would dissolve these objections because he was focusing her upon one main objection — that she was too heavy to sit upon the boy. When this was the only issue, he proposed that she would find she was hardly heavy enough to hold the boy down and would appreciate having the weight (he was also working on her obesity problem). She didn't believe this was so and wished to prove him wrong. Yet the only way she could prove him wrong was to sit upon the boy; when she did, she found she needed all of her weight.

If an issue of winning becomes too important to a patient, Erickson is also willing to let a patient defeat him; once the patient has won, he will be willing to go along with Erickson on other issues which lead to change.

It is Erickson's ability to find solutions, compromises, and ideas to resolve apparently insoluble dilemmas which makes him appear so clever in his work with patients. Therapists who wish to adopt his approach often feel they could not think of the solutions which apparently come so easily to him. Yet if one attempts Erickson's approach, similar kinds of ideas begin to seem obvious ways of solving problems. The solutions follow as one begins to grasp the premises about therapy which are the basis of this approach.

Use of Anecdotes

Although he does not seem to have written about it, Erickson uses stories and anecdotes when dealing with his patients. He teaches by analogies which are related to the patient's problem in some way, although often in a way that the patient cannot easily discover. These anecdotes may be personal experiences, happenings with past patients, or stories and jokes that are part of the shared culture of Erickson and his patients. Like any good teacher, he puts over ideas with parables, particularly ideas which cannot be communicated in more straightforward ways. At times, he uses stories and anecdotes to "peg" an idea so the patient will not forget it or will accept a possibility which was previously unacceptable. For example, he will sometimes suggest that a person can stop a lifelong habit in a matter of seconds just because of an idea. Then he will report the experience of an orderly in a hospital who had been accustomed to drinking a milkshake at lunch every day for over twenty years. One day while he was making his usual milkshake, a nurse pointed out to him that the supply of cow's milk had not been available for several days and he had been making his daily milkshake with mother's milk. He set the milkshake down and never drank another for lunch, changing a habit of many years duration. Yet all that had changed was the introduction of an idea since the difference in the drink was undetectable.

However, it should be emphasized that Erickson's therapy does not consist largely of discussion or teaching in the usual sense. He combines discussion and action, with the action taking place both in the room and outside of it in the social arena.

Willingness to Release Patients

Although he will take responsibility and direct patients what to do, Erickson does not seem concerned about the patient becoming overdependent upon him. The framework he establishes in the therapeutic relationship has built into it the idea that the relationship is temporary to achieve particular ends. Since he does not use "awareness" of the relationship as a way of keeping the patient a distance from himself, both he and the patient can become intensely involved. Yet a part of the paradox of his approach is the way he manages to begin termination with the moment of contact, and future disengagement is part of the intensity of the relationship established. Because of his positive view and his respect for patients, Erickson is willing to start a change and then release the patient to let the change develop further. He does not allow the needs of the treatment setting to perpetuate the patient's distress, as can happen in long term therapy. Since he does not see therapy as a total clearance, or cure, of all the patient's present and future problems, he is willing to give patients up. His approach is to remove obstacles which, once removed, allow the patient to develop his career in his own way. The process of termination also becomes a part of the natural course of treatment with Erickson, since he is willing to shift to irregular sessions and recess treatment for periods of time. By recessing and having later follow-up sessions, he continues to be important in the patient's life while allowing the patient the freedom to progress.

THE THEORY OF THIS APPROACH

It should be evident to the reader that the therapeutic approach briefly described here does not fit into the usual theories of psychopathology and therapeutic change. There is a discontinuity between the usual way of thinking about therapy and Erickson's approach.

While Erickson was working out his methods, two major theoretical schemes were developed in psychiatry and psychology. These were psychoanalytic theory and conditioning theory. Although they differ in many ways, both of these theories share a number of premises about psychopathology:

1. The unit of observation and treatment is the individual.
2. The primary area of concern is the past of the individual. His current situation is of secondary, if not minor, importance as an influence on his behavior. In the psychoanalytic view, the individual is an expression of the infantile neurosis and past traumas which have produced, and continue to have a dynamic influence upon, his perception and behavior. In conditioning theory, the person's current behavior is a product of his past conditioning, which is now built into neurological processes.
3. What an individual says and does is conceived as a report about the processes within him. His symptoms are maladaptive expressions of his unconscious dynamic conflicts or his conditioned ways of perceiving and behaving.
4. The theoretical problem is to devise metaphors about the processes within the individual which best explain the way he is behaving.

Given this way of defining the psychiatric arena, the goals and techniques of therapy inevitably follow. The therapeutic goal must be to change the processes within the person. In psychoanalysis, the therapist seeks to change the person's unconscious dynamics, and in conditioning therapy he seeks to inhibit previous conditioning and develop new percepts. The conditioning therapist attempts to inhibit previous conditioned responses with drugs or reciprocal inhibition procedures, or he tries to condition new responses and suppress old ones with verbal conditioning procedures. In psychoanalysis, the patient is given insight into his unconscious ideation, and repressions are lifted as transference distortions are interpreted to him.

Because the therapeutic problem was defined in this way, a rather grandiose idea about therapy developed in psychiatry. Implicit in therapy based upon psychoanalytic and conditioning theory is the idea that successful treatment will "clear" the individual of his problems and he will have no more difficulties the remainder of his life. When the influence of the past is resolved, the individual will no longer be neurotic or psychotic and will deal successfully with all problems of living. Any treatment which does less than this is said to be mere transference cure, social amelioration, suppression of symptoms, or supportive therapy. Unique to psychoanalysis is the idea that the longer the treatment the more successful the treatment, and brief treatment must by definition be inadequate.

The chief merit of these theories is that they are coherent within their premises and they have been sufficiently worked out to be a body of teachable theory. The chief demerit is their basic assumption that the individual lives alone and autonomously and is not responding to other people in his current situation. Consequently there is no appreciation, or even awareness, of the influence of the patient's social network, nor is there any awareness of the consequences to his intimates when the patient changes. Since the unit is the single individual, the theoretical framework does not allow a description of both therapist and patient in the interchange. A final demerit, which applies particularly to psychoanalysis, is the fact that evidence to support the claims that "deep" long-term therapy produces any therapeutic change has never been provided.

Whatever the merits of these traditional theories or the treatment which follows from them, they are largely irrelevant when one wishes to describe the therapy of Erickson. Examining what he does with a patient, it is clear that his unit of observation is not the single individual, nor is he particularly concerned about the past of the patient. He is concerned about the current situation, and he approaches symptoms as ways the patient adapts to that situation. He does not see symptomatic behavior as merely a report about the person's inner state; it is also a way the person is dealing with other people, including himself. He does not approach patients with the idea that he can "clear" them so they can deal with all future problems. Instead, he sees therapy as a way of intervening into the life of a patient in difficulty in such a way that the patient recovers from his current dilemma and is hopefully shifted to a more successful level of functioning in the real world. In his usual practice, Erickson does not use the de-conditioning procedures of reciprocal inhibition or use verbal conditioning procedures, nor does he encourage insight into unconscious processes or make transference interpretations. What Erickson does in therapy is based upon a different set of premises about what psychopathology is and what should be done about it. These premises have not yet been put within a coherent theory, nor will they be until someone provides a theoretical model which describes the processes which occur between people. Erickson has provided a necessary first step in the development of an interpersonal theory by working out operational procedure for inducing changes in the ways people deal with one another.

What Erickson has provided can be illustrated with an idea from communications theory. Gregory Bateson once proposed that every expression of an individual, or message from him, can be viewed as both a report and a command. The person who says "I feel unhappy" is reporting on his state. He is also commanding or directing or influencing the person with whom he is talking, if only by indicating "treat me as a person who feels unhappy." Because traditional psychiatry and psychology only placed one person in the field of observation, only the report aspect of the message was noticed. When a person said "I am afraid," his statement was taken only as a report about his condition. The theoretical problem was to construct an explanation of his state. As another example, if a person put his hand over his mouth while speaking, he might be described as someone expressing an unconscious desire not to speak. Words or actions of a person were taken as reports, essentially as clues, about the perceptual and affective processes within him.

What Erickson has added is an emphasis upon the "command" aspect of a message as well as the "report." He assumes a person's statement is addressed to another person and both people should be included in the description. When a hypnotic subject reports that his hand feels light, he is not merely reporting a sensation; in Erickson's view he is also making a statement about cooperation or resistance to the person hypnotizing him. The patient who behaves in an agitated way and says he is too nervous to sit down is not merely reporting upon his state. He is also commanding, or influencing, the therapist to deal with him in particular ways. Because of his way of conceiving human behavior, Erickson's treatment cannot be adequately described within psychoanalytic or conditioning theory because the more narrow focus of those views is limited to the single individual.

There are ideas derived from conditioning theory which are appropriate for describing Erickson's therapeutic approach, but only if one broadens the focus. To Erickson, stimuli are never single; there is not a stimulus and a response nor a single reinforcement. There are always multiple responses and multiple reinforcements all occurring simultaneously and often conflictual in nature. As he has put it, a person can say "no" so that it means "yes, no, maybe, or I wonder if you mean that." Every message is always qualified in multiple ways. Similarly, he tends to think in terms of conditioning a situation rather than an individual. If he can start a wife responding differently to her husband, the husband will in turn respond differently to her, and a new system of interchange will have begun which will continue. This is conditioning by arranging new reinforcements, but to encompass what he does in this framework, one must expand the meaning of those terms to include multiple levels and a social network.

When one reads Erickson's works, he will find that words which have a traditional meaning within a framework of individual theory have a different meaning the way Erickson uses them. For example, the word "symptom" is traditionally used to mean an expression of an unconscious conflict, a manifestation in behavior of something with roots in intrapsychic life. Erickson, in his later writing, tends to use "symptom" to refer to a kind of behavior which is socially adaptive and which is in itself the difficulty of the patient. The symptom is assumed to have a social function and the goal is to change the symptomatic behavior rather than what is supposedly "behind" it. If a symptom has "roots," they are in the social network.

Another term Erickson has re-defined is "hypnosis." Traditionally, hypnosis was the state of an individual. The focus was upon the suggestibility of the subject, his depth of trance, and so on. What Erickson has done is include both subject and hypnotist in the description. When he speaks of "hypnosis," he is not merely referring to the processes within a subject but to the type of interchange between two people. Consequently, his emphasis is upon the hypnotist gaining cooperation from the subject, dealing with resistant behavior, receiving acknowledgement that something is happening, and so on. It is this broader definition of hypnosis which makes it difficult at times to tell whether Erickson hypnotized a patient or not. He used a type of interchange which he considers hypnotic, although no formal induction of hypnosis in the traditional sense was conducted. His introduction of two people into the definition of hypnosis requires a new formulation of that age-old phenomenon.

A more extreme example of his re-definition, or re-conceptualization, of a term is the way he uses the term "unconscious." The unconscious, by definition, has always been a term which applied to one person — a something within that person. Erickson does not view the "unconscious" that way, with a consequent effect upon his therapeutic procedures.

The idea of the unconscious came largely out of the hypnotic investigations in the last quarter of the 19th century. When a subject in trance followed suggestions and could not explain why he was doing what he was doing, it was necessary to postulate a motivating force inside the person which was outside his awareness. Freud carried this idea further with a hypothesis that the unconscious was a part of the mind containing dynamic instinctual forces which determined the ideas and behavior of a person. Freud was also interested in the common language, or logic, of the unconscious of different people. Jung too postulated a similarity in the unconscious of different individuals with his idea of the collective unconscious.

I believe that Erickson in his set of premises has shifted the traditional view of the unconscious. He began by exploring unconscious ideation and the differences between conscious thought processes and unconscious thought processes. An example of this view is in "The Use of Automatic Drawing in the Interpretation and Relief of a State of Acute Obsessional Depression." He then went a step further to consider whether one person's unconscious could read and interpret the productions of another person's unconscious. With Lawrence Kubie, he wrote "The Translation of Cryptic Automatic Writing of One Hypnotic Subject by Another in a Trance Like

Dissociated State." They say in that paper, commenting on the fact that one person could decipher accurately the automatic writing of another, "The observation stresses from a new angle a fact that has often been emphasized by those who have studied unconscious processes but which remains none the less mysterious — namely, that underneath the diversified nature of the consciously organized aspects of the personality, the unconscious talks in a language which has a remarkable uniformity; furthermore that that language has laws so constant that the unconscious of one individual is better equipped to understand the unconscious of another than the conscious aspect of the personality of either."

The next step for Erickson was, I believe, to assume that the language of the unconscious was not merely expressive — a report of what was on the person's mind. It was also a way of communicating *to* another person. That is, we communicate with a conscious language and we also communicate to one another with an unconscious language which we understand and respond to. This unconscious language is in a different code; there is condensation, no sense of time, and so on. The communication is in the form of body movement, vocal intonation, and the metaphors and analogies implicit in our verbal speech.

If one assumes that Erickson operates on the premise that there are at least two levels of communication, one of them crudely called conscious communication and another equally crudely called unconscious communication, then many of the ways he operates become more understandable. He considers an ability to read unconscious communication an essential skill in a therapist. His own ability to consciously receive kinesic communication is legendary. He likes to point out how important it is that a therapist be able to note when a patient nods or shakes the head in contradiction to the spoken words, or the way a woman covers her purse with a scarf while appearing to give full information, or the innumerable non-verbal communications of all kinds. Routinely, he says, a married female patient will disclose she is having an affair by her way of sitting down in the chair at the first interview, and she does it the same way whatever her social class. However, Erickson does not offer interpretations which attempt to bring the unconscious language into consciousness; he treats them as two different styles of communication, each of which is acceptable. In fact, what he seems to mean by "accepting" the patient is an acceptance of this multicommunication style of relating. He would not, for example, point out to a patient that putting his hand over his mouth is an unconscious way of indicating he does not want to talk about something. Instead, Erickson accepts that movement as the patient's quite adequate way of telling him something. To bring the movement to the patient's attention would disrupt the communication and not lead to a benefical result. In fact, it could cause a patient to try to be aware of ways of communicating which function best outside conscious awareness.

To Erickson, it is reasonable to talk to a patient about one thing while simultaneously communicating about quite different matters. For example, he will give an academic lecture while simultaneously hypnotizing a particular person in the audience, or he will talk about seemingly trivial matters with a patient while simultaneously carrying on through body movement and vocal intonation a conversation about the important concerns of the patient. Many of the body movements which a therapist uses "naturally" are used deliberately by Erickson, such as postural shifts, focusing his body in relation to the patient, or changing levels of his voice to bring about responsive body movement. He uses verbal communication as only one of the many possible ways of communicating, and with hypnotic subjects who did not speak English, he has demonstrated that trance can be induced entirely by non-verbal behavior.

Erickson's comments about "unconscious awareness" become reasonable from this view. To have an interchange with another person through an "unconscious means of communication, we must at some level be cognizant of what we are doing or we could not correct ourselves or receive the other person's communication and respond to it. Yet this process can go on without any conscious awareness of what we were doing. Therefore there must be, at least, two levels of "awareness" when we are interchanging two levels, at least, of communication. What is most distinctive about Erickson is his willingness to allow the separate existence of these levels without attempting to call the patient's attention to them. Erickson is willing to communicate in both codes and leave them both functioning separately in the interchange.

The Cause of Therapeutic Change

Implicit in Erickson's way of working with patients is the idea that a psychiatric problem is interpersonal in nature. The ways the patient deals with other people and they with him produces his feelings of distress and restricted ways of behaving. Given this view, the problem of how to change the person becomes one of how to change his relationships with others, including the therapist. Past theories about the "cause" of therapeutic change do not apply when the problem is conceived in this way. Somewhere in his career, Erickson deviated quite sharply from the belief that a person will change if he learns why he is the way he is or what is "behind" his problem. It is not possible to understand his therapeutic approach by thinking of therapy as a process of bringing unconscious ideas into awareness or of helping the person understand how he deals with others. Erickson does not help the patient understand the relation of his past to his present, nor does he help him understand why he is the way he is or how he relates to other people. His case reports do not include statements which are typical of many therapists, such as, "Let's try to get some understanding of what's behind this," or "Have you noticed that you talk about her in the same way you discuss your mother?" or "You seem to be reacting to me like I'm someone else," or "How do you feel about that?" or "You seem angry." His approach does not involve making the person stand off and examine what he is saying and doing (unless the patient really wants such an experience, and then Erickson might provide it quite vividly with hypnotic techniques). Should a patient behave toward him as if he is a magical, powerful person, Erickson does not point this out to the patient. He might make use of the behavior to induce a change, or he might shift the patient's behavior so that he responds differently, but he seems to assume that attempting to make the person more aware would not be helpful. One consequence of his approach is that his ex-patients do not speak the language of psychiatry or think in that ideology. Nor do they use psychiatric interpretations on other people. They achieve normality with no more concern about insight than the average untreated person.

One argument is often offered for the necessity of insight or understanding. It is said that therapeutic change will not persist after treatment without it. There is no evidence for this belief and considerable evidence that change without insight persists. It seems to be Erickson's view that when a person changes, his social situation changes, and the persistence of change is related to the new situation which has been created.

Many contemporary therapists have come to believe that therapy is an "experience" which is in itself causal to change. They may phrase it as an experience of intimacy with another human being, an experience of discovering their places in an existential world, an awareness of new depths of perception through an L.S.D. experience, and so on. Erickson does not seem to view an experience in itself as relevant to change. Although patients will have an experience with him, and often an intense one, it is only productive if it provokes, and directly leads to, a change in the person's daily living.

One theoretical model which seems appropriate for Erickson's therapy is that of teacher and student, yet to say this is to attempt to explain one unknown with another, since we do not know much about the process of teaching which induces basic changes in the student. If one thinks of teaching as a process of transmitting information, the model is not appropriate. Thinking of it as a process of developing changes in the teacher's relationship with a student, the model becomes more useful. Erickson teaches a patient to deal with him, and with other people, differently. He does this largely by blocking off the ways the person typically behaves, and simultaneously he provides him with new experiences which prove more successful and satisfying. Quite typically he leads the patient into discovering that what he thought he did not know he already knows. A favorite example of Erickson's is the woman who could not learn to write despite the attempt of many people to teach her. Erickson taught her to make various lines which she was quite capable of making, such as straight lines, circles, half circles, and so on. He then had her put them together and discover that she already knew how to write the letters of the alphabet. It is characteristic of Erickson's teaching that he does not tell the patient what he ought to know; he arranges a situation where the person's own experience validates what he has learned. For example, Erickson once described a case in which a husband benevolently made all the decisions for his wife, imposing a kind of tyranny which produced in the wife only resistance and ingratitude. When Erickson was asked why he did not point out to the husband that this was happening, he replied that there would be no point in explaining the situation to the husband, he wouldn't understand it. By arranging a situation where the husband allowed the wife her own way, Erickson managed to provide the husband with a response from the wife which he had never had before so that he learned to prefer to treat his wife differently.

A key factor in understanding Erickson's therapy is to realize that he does not assume therapeutic change occurs as a result of more awareness or knowledge in the usual sense. He does not teach the patient what he should know. Instead, he arranges a situation which necessarily requires new behavior from the person and consequently a different experience of living. He seems to assume that man is not basically a rational animal but a learning organism which only learns through the action of an experience.

If one takes these many aspects of Erickson's therapy and puts them together, a general approach to treatment appears. He approaches each new patient with an expectation that a unique treatment operation might be appropriate for this particular person and situation. He also assumes a range of possible therapeutic settings; he might work in the office, in the home, or in the place of business. He might see the patient for an hour or for several hours, charge one type of fee or another, and do either brief or long-term therapy. His attitude toward the new patient is an expectancy that the patient will naturally improve when obstacles holding him back are removed. He is willing to take full responsibility for what is to happen with the patient and also willing to decline that responsibility if appropriate. In the first encounter, he accepts what the patient has to offer and defines the relationship as one in which he is willing to work within a framework the patient can already understand. He moves as rapidly as possible toward a change; his moves are to offer alternative experiences, provoke the patient into action which requires new behavior, and move to block off symptomatic behavior which has been restricting the patient. He makes maximum use of the way the patient deals with other people. When he has started changes developing in the patient's life, he is willing to release the patient so that he has the opportunity for further development in his own autonomous way.

This summary of Erickson's approach has been phrased in the most general way, partly because it is difficult to be specific about what he does without pointing to the details of cases he has written up and lectured about. Each case is unique. Another difficulty in generalizing about Erickson is that inevitably there seems to be an exception to whatever one says. He will go to considerable trouble to emphasize that fact about his work. Once many years ago, a research investigator was engaging in long conversations with Erickson to obtain generalizations about his theraputic procedures. The young man wanted clear statements about his "method" and Erickson was doing his best to educate him. At a certain point Erickson interrupted the discussion and took the young man outside the house to the front lawn. He pointed up the street and asked what he saw. Puzzled, the young man replied that he saw a street. Erickson asked if he saw anything else. When he continued to be puzzled, Erickson pointed to the trees which lined the street. "Do you notice anything about those trees?" he asked. After a period of study, the young man said they all were leaning in an easterly direction. "That's right," said Erickson, pleased. "All except one. That second one from the end is leaning in a westerly direction. There's always an exception."

At the time of that incident, I thought that Erickson was going to excessive trouble to make a point; yet now whenever I attempt to simplify complex processes, particularly when describing Erickson's work, the experience in Phoenix that afternoon comes vividly to mind.

3

Erickson's Contribution
to Therapy
(1982)

I will present some personal experience with Milton Erickson and try to communicate some of my understanding of this extraordinary man and his work. I have published my views of Erickson's therapy extensively, but to me he remains a mysterious person. Although I met with him for many years, I never fully understood him. In hundreds of hours talking together, I explored his life and work; yet I know him less well than other men I have associated with more briefly. I studied a number of therapists over the years, and Erickson more extensively than anyone. Having learned many of his therapy techniques, I applied them in my practice and teaching. Not a day passes that I do not use something that I learned from Erickson in my work. Yet his basic ideas I only partially grasp. I feel that if I understood more fully what Erickson was trying to explain about changing people, new innovations in therapy would open up before me.

Erickson was by no means secretive about his work. Quite possibly he was the most visible therapist the world has ever known. For many years he gave seminars and workshops to large audiences in this country and abroad. He wrote over one hundred publications. Thousands of visitors came to talk with him, individually and in groups. His lectures, demonstrations, and conversations have been recorded more than those of any other clinician. He gave generously of himself and his knowledge to anyone who was interested. Although Erickson liked to show you that you still had much to learn, he did not attempt to be mysterious or obscure. He really tried to simplify and explain his ideas so everyone could understand them. Often he was frustrated when his ideas were only partially understood by many of us. I don't know how many times over the years I asked him why he did something in therapy and he answered, "That's obvious." I would say, "Milton, it's not obvious," and I pursued him only to find a new and unexpected complexity in his thinking.

It was not only the unusual nature of his ideas that made Erickson difficult to fully understand. One problem was the way he talked with people. Erickson tended to join the person he was talking with in that person's language. His style of therapy and teaching was to converse in the language of the other person; within that framework he suggested new ideas. This style of "accepting" the person's language as a way of joining gave professionals with quite incompatible theories the idea that Erickson operated within their ways of thinking. He could talk in many ideological languages, so that colleagues and patients often had the illusion they shared and understood his theories and were later surprised by an unexpected idea. Erickson's own beliefs and premises about therapy were not self-evident. When one asked him about a theory, the response was often a case example which was a metaphor with many referents.

Erickson's use of stories in his conversations gave people of diverse views metaphors where they discovered their own ideas. Each anecdote was put in such a way that quite different people thought it was designed precisely for them. When some of my trainees visited Phoenix and met with Erickson in a group, they returned and reported on the experience. One of them mentioned a story that Erickson had told about him. One of the others said no, that story was actually about *her.* Yet another said the other two did not understand that the story applied to his particular experience. It turned out that all of the group thought they had each received a personal metaphor from Erickson designed just for them. Each felt that he or she had been understood by Erickson and really understood him. Yet they were people of quite diverse backgrounds and perspectives, and the metaphors were stories and cases that Erickson had told many times before (although his way of telling the story would vary). Some of the stories were ones I had heard many years before and I knew they applied personally to me.

The fact that Erickson talked on many different levels of meaning at the same time also complicated the problem of getting a flat statement of his views. When asked what to do with a therapeutic problem, Erickson would offer advice and usually a case illustration to show how he dealt with a similar problem. Yet that case example was not merely a description of a case. It might also be a metaphor designed to change or resolve some personal problem of the person he was talking with. That is, Erickson could talk about a case in a way that educated one about the general nature of that problem, taught how to use a particular therapy technique, and encouraged or imposed a change in one's personal life or ideas.

One of Erickson's greatest skills was his ability to influence people indirectly. This is one of the reasons so many people were uneasy in his presence. Anyone talking with Erickson could never be quite sure whether he was only offering professional advice or subtly suggesting a change in an unstated personal problem. A story or a case example is an analogy drawing a parallel between one situation and another. While the case example would pair a therapy technique and a problem, it could also be an analogy in relation to the person being talked with and the person in the case example. Erickson liked to change people outside their awareness. If they were on guard against his influence and resisted the idea Erickson was offering, it was usually some other idea that Erickson was actually interested in imposing. He liked to offer an idea to resist and one to influence, at least.

Erickson would tell the same case example in different ways to different people. While the essentials of the case remained the same, what he emphasized in the complex story would vary with the analogy he was communicating to that particular listener. This complex process of metaphoric influence could occur routinely while Erickson was in conversation with people or while he was doing a case consultation. It was as if doing one thing at a time bored him, and he needed to communicate in more complex ways.

What Erickson said and did had multiple purposes and he taught in complex analogies. Therefore, it is difficult to say flatly that a particular idea or technique was his view. His theory was offered to us in metaphors with many referents, told with different analogies, emphasized in different ways for different people, and varying with the social context.

A major difficulty in grasping what was new in Erickson's theories is the problem of language. He was talking about new premises about human beings and ways to change them in a language constructed to express past views. (One is reminded of Harry Stack Sullivan, who struggled to describe interpersonal relations in a language constructed for describing individuals.) I think Erickson was offering something new in the world—a presentation of the intricacies of interpersonal influence (at least that was the set of ideas he talked to me about). Yet he had available only a language developed for a quite different conception of people. The language for describing an individual is simply not adequate to describe Erickson's therapy.

I think the language of hypnosis and hypnotherapy is too primitive and limited to encompass the complexities of many of Erickson's trance inductions and his use of hypnotic influence in therapy. How can one talk about a hypnotic induction in the language of "sleep" when the subject is hypnotized while walking up and down the room? Or how can one talk about the complex interpersonal influence of a conversational trance induction in the language of the "unconscious"? As an example, Erickson attempted to explain the fact that if a subject followed the directive to have a negative hallucination, he must see the object in order to avoid seeing it. Erickson sometimes used the term "unconscious awareness" to describe this phenomenon. Yet the term "unconscious" is by definition something outside of consciousness, or awareness.

Clearly such terminology is too cumbersome to explain the subtle processes which interested Erickson. He was elaborating a new way of thinking about people, about hypnosis, and about therapy without a descriptive language that could express that new view. It was like trying to talk about quantum theory in a language of levers and weights. I believe that is why he turned more and more to metaphor, which is not a way to describe an idea rigorously but it can cover the complexity he was trying to communicate.

Many people here today never met Erickson. Others are so young they saw him only in his old age. Granting that he was a formidable man even when old and frail and in a wheelchair, I would like to communicate something of what he was like in his middle years when he was vigorous.* I think his success as a therapist was partly the result of the personal power that exuded from him. Not only did his personality have an impact, but his power was increased by his reputation as a hypnotist who influenced

---

*Many people think of Erickson as an old man who was frail and spoke with extreme difficulty. I think that is unfortunate. In his prime he had more control of his vocal inflections and his body movement than anyone I knew. That was part of his mastery of skills in influencing people. He had extraordinary ability to communicate with others. There is too little visual record of that skill remaining. Some years ago I asked him about videotaping his work, and he said he would rather not allow it. He did not want to be remembered as a helpless old man who communicated with difficulty. Finally, he allowed that videotaping, and so, many people only know him in his frail period and do not have any idea what he was like at the height of his power.

people outside their awareness. Quite a number of people were simply afraid of him.

I discovered Erickson's power when I first heard of him in 1953. While on Gregory Bateson's research project on communication, I told Bateson that I would like to take a workshop being offered by a hypnotist coming to San Francisco. I wanted to study the communicative aspects of hypnosis. Bateson asked me who was giving the workshop, and I told him it was Milton H. Erickson. "I'll call him," said Bateson, "and ask if you can attend." In that way I found out that Bateson knew Erickson, just as he seemed to know anyone of importance in the social science field. It turned out that Bateson and Margaret Mead had consulted with Erickson and Mrs. Erickson about the films of trance dances they had made in Bali. They were consulting to determine when the dancers in masks went into trance. (In fact, it was Bateson and Mead who encouraged Erickson to publish that extraordinary description of communication he wrote up in "A Study of an Experimental Neurosis Hypnotically Induced in a Case of Ejaculatio Praecox.")

Bateson called Erickson at his hotel in San Francisco (we were in Menlo Park) and asked if I could attend the workshop. Erickson said I was welcome. They chatted awhile, and Bateson hung up the telephone and said, "That man is going to manipulate me to come to San Francisco and have dinner with him." Interested in manipulation, I asked, "What did he say to you?" Bateson replied, "He said to me, 'Why don't you come to San Francisco and have dinner with me?'" Even straightforward statements by Erickson were suspect with Gregory Bateson and with other people who feared his power.

Erickson clearly enjoyed his reputation as a powerful person who influenced people both in and outside their awareness. I recall that once our project was having an evening seminar with Erickson, and Don D. Jackson was present. As we were discussing hypnosis, Jackson was holding a pencil in one hand and turning it round and round. Jackson said, "I can't stop turning this pencil, and Milton, I think you have something to do with it." "Well," replied Erickson, "you can continue to turn the pencil." He proceeded to give Jackson a few suggestions and then he had him stop the turning. Later I asked Erickson privately just what he said to Jackson that made him turn the pencil that way. I wanted more information about his ways of inducing special behavior in someone while ostensibly merely having a conversation. "I didn't have anything to do with it," said Erickson.

"But Jackson seemed to think I was doing something, so I took advantage of that."

To illustrate another aspect of Erickson's formidability as a hypnotist and a person, let me describe an incident which truly impressed me and John Weakland. One evening we took the Ericksons out to dinner to a Mexican restaurant on one of our visits here. It was an authentic type of Mexican restaurant, as I learned when I put some of their standard hot sauce on my food. I gasped and my eyes watered uncontrollably. Erickson kidded me about that. Somehow out of the conversation came Erickson's claim that he could survive any hot sauce that could be served to him. To demonstrate, he called the waitress and sent her for the chef. He asked the Mexican chef to put together the hottest sauce he could make in the kitchen and deliver it to the table. The chef seemed pleased with the challenge. He came back in a little while with something in a small dish and he placed it before Erickson. He stayed to watch him eat it, with some anticipation. Erickson took a spoon, dipped it into the hot sauce, and then put it in his mouth and rolled it around his tongue. His face did not change expression, nor did his eyes show the slightest sign of watering. "Delicious," he said. I was impressed — and even more impressed when I watched the astonishment of that Mexican chef.

Besides his skill in influencing people, there was simply something about Erickson that made him difficult to oppose. I recall a psychiatrist telling me about an experience with Erickson here in Phoenix. The psychiatrist was a mature, responsible man with an important position in the field. He told me that Erickson spent an eight-hour day with him, and the psychiatrist said he never had lunch because Erickson did not. He told me that he got so hungry. I asked him why he did not tell Erickson he was hungry and wanted some lunch. He said that somehow he felt he could not say that to Erickson while he was busy instructing him about therapy. Months later he was still angry at having gone hungry like that. I told him that Erickson must have thought he was important. He didn't often spend eight hours with a visitor, so it was quite a compliment. That pleased the psychiatrist and seemed to help make up for the lost lunch.

Erickson was always quite comfortable with power. He did not mind taking it or using it. I recall his saying that he was on a panel and "there was no power there, so I took over the panel." With his willingness to take and use power, I think it is fortunate that he was a benevolent man. If the kind of influence he had was turned to destructive purposes, it would have been most unfortunate. Erickson was not only benevolent, but he was consistently helpful to people, both in and out of his office.

I spend my time restraining therapists from being helpful. I don't believe benevolent helpfulness should be imposed on people, and therapy should not be done unless people have clearly requested it. Yet somehow I was never concerned with that issue with Erickson. He would set out to change whomever he thought ought to be changed whether they had requested that in any direct way or not. I never had a doubt about his ethics or benevolent intentions, nor was I concerned about his exploiting anyone for any personal advantage.

A similar issue arises about using individuals or families for demonstration purposes before audiences. I have been opposed to using people for teaching purposes because I think it exploits them. Yet I was never concerned about that issue with Erickson. He not only used people to demonstrate for large crowds at his workshops, but he also did helpful therapy with them before that audience while he was demonstrating hypnosis. He always managed it so that the subject got a fair exchange of benefits for being used in the demonstration. He also protected the person so that changes he was inducing were not even known to the audience. He had the ability, through his extraordinary use of language, to have a private exchange with a subject while doing a public demonstration.

Although Erickson condemned stage hypnosis, he was really a great performer himself at hypnotic demonstrations. He could simultaneously teach a hypnotic technique, give therapy to a subject, illustrate a point at issue with a colleague, and entertain the audience. The speed with which he worked could be the envy of any stage practitioner.

As an example, I recall a demonstration Erickson once did before a large audience. He asked for a volunteer and a young man came up and sat down with him. Erickson's only trance induction was to ask the young man to put his hands on his knees. Then he said, "Would you be willing to continue to see your hands on your knees?" The young man said he would. While talking with him, Erickson gestured to a colleague on the other side of the young man, and the colleague lifted up the young man's arm and it remained in the air. Erickson said to the young man, "How many hands do you have?" "Two, of course," said the young man. "I'd like you to count them as I point to them," said Erickson. "All right," said the young man, in a rather patronizing way. Erickson pointed to the hand on one knee, and the young man said, "One." Erickson pointed to the vacant other knee, where the young man had agreed to continue to see his hand, and the young man said, "Two." Then Erickson pointed to the hand up in the air. The young man stared at it, puzzled. "How do you explain that other hand?" asked Erickson. "I don't know," said the young man. "I guess I should be in a circus." That hypnotic induction took about as long as it took me to describe it here.

It was always a pleasure to watch Erickson do one of his stage demonstrations. Some of his most interesting ones were his demonstrations of dealing with resistance to hypnosis. He would begin by asking for a volunteer to come up from the audience and be resistant. As always with Erickson, he was managing it so that if the person was resistant he was cooperating.

Erickson enjoyed showing that inducing a trance could not be described simply. He illustrated the many ways it could be done. I recall one demonstration where he showed that one could induce a trance without saying a word. He asked a resistant subject to come up on stage and a young man came up. Erickson just stood there saying and doing nothing. I could see the young man going into a trance. Later I asked Erickson what subtle thing he did to bring that about. He said he induced a trance by *not* doing anything. The young man came up in front of all those people to be hypnotized and Erickson did not do anything. "Somebody had to do something," said Erickson, "so the young man went into a trance."

I am reminded of my neophyte days when I was learning to use hypnosis in therapy. I would have a patient sit down and I would go through an induction procedure. I began to notice that a number of patients went into a trance when they first sat down in the chair in my office. What I was doing was waking them up so I could hypnotize them. I began to realize, and I think it was after that demonstration by Erickson, that when people came to be hypnotized it was not necessary to do more than get out of their way. Erickson used the social context when doing hypnosis and always thought in a larger unit than just himself and the subject. Hypnotic subjects are often better subjects on stage when in a triangle with the audience than when in a dyad alone with the hypnotist.

Besides his power to influence people outside awareness, Erickson had another ability which made some people uneasy in his company. He was an extraordinary observer and could just about read a person's mind from his or her posture and body movement. He put great emphasis on the therapist being an acute observer, treating posture and responsive movement as a language in itself.

Erickson liked to improve a trainee's ability to observe. Once when John Weakland and I visited, he called us into his office briefly to look at a patient. It was a woman sitting in a chair with her eyes closed. Later, when the woman had left, Erickson asked us what we had observed. The question was so general that we found it difficult to answer. We made wise comments, such as the fact that we noticed it was a woman and even that she was in a trance. Erickson dismissed our observations and pointed out that one half of the woman's face was slightly larger than the other half and her right hand was slightly larger than her left. He said that was obviously important for diagnosis and we had to agree.

Generally people do not choose to be closely observed; trainees of Erickson were uneasy with his skill in observation. I once spent some time talking with a psychiatrist who had been a psychiatric resident in training with Erickson in Michigan many years before. He told me about the residents' respect, if not fear, of Erickson. He said that Erickson had high expectations of a student — he would pose a question and then stare at the resident with what they called his "ocular fix." His powers of observation, which he insisted the residents develop, were becoming legendary. For example, this psychiatrist told me that one day his wife was walking across the hospital grounds and Erickson stopped her. "You're pregnant, aren't you?" he said. "Yes," she said, surprised because she had just learned the fact herself. "How did you know?" she asked. Erickson said, "Your forehead has changed color."

Erickson had high expectations of himself as a clinician and held the same expectations of trainees. He expected a therapist to be an acute observer, but more than that he expected a wide range of skills. He would emphasize how a therapist should use his own movement and posture to influence a patient. Often he would illustrate with a head movement or another body movement how one should offer an idea with special emphasis. He also expected a therapist to control his voice so that words could be given special emphasis when an idea was being communicated. He liked to say a sentence and put emphasis on certain words so that he was communicating a different sentence by that emphasis. When discussing how he phrased something to a patient, Erickson would duplicate the vocal emphasis he had used. Sometimes the differences he was emphasizing were so subtle they were difficult to grasp.

Erickson expected a clinician to have a thorough knowledge of types of psychopathology, a broad understanding of human beings and their normal social situations, common sense, keen observation, and an ability to use the self in a wide range of ways from being authoritative to being helpless. He also expected a therapist to have an actor's control of his use of body movement and vocal intonation. After observing Erickson, I began to realize what abilities were necessary to become a master therapist. At that time I began to think about turning to a less exacting profession, like being a supervisor or teacher.

One of the most important aspects of Erickson that permeated his work was his sense of humor. He found humor everywhere and enjoyed practical jokes and puzzles as well as puns and turns of phrase. It was his humor that saved him, I think, from being overwhelming in his power. Something about the absurd nature of human beings and their problems was taken for granted by him. Let me give an example. I once consulted him about a case of a young couple. The wife was exasperated by her husband following her around wherever she went, particularly when she did housework on the weekends. If she went into the kitchen, he went into the kitchen, and if she went outside, he went outside. Her main objection was his following her from room to room and watching her when she vacuumed the house. She had protested to him, and he said he tried to stop, but somehow he could not. He found himself following her around and watching her vacuum.

I asked Erickson what I might do to solve the problem with this couple. He said the solution was obvious. I should talk privately with the wife and get her to agree to follow my instructions. The next Saturday she should vacuum as usual, and when her husband followed her from room to room she should make no comment. After she finished vacuuming, she should take the bag full of dirt and go back to each room where she had vacuumed and make a pile of dirt on the floor. She should say, "Well, that's that," and not touch that dirt until she vacuumed the following Saturday so that it remained there all week. I instructed the wife as Erickson suggested. Her husband stopped following her around the house.

The therapy of Erickson, more than that of any other therapist, seems to force us to consider whether the map of logic is the appropriate one to explain the behavior and dilemmas of human beings. He lived quite comfortably with paradox, while most people try to avoid that. When he could, he framed his actions in paradoxical ways. Let me cite an example from one of Erickson's social experiments.

A unique aspect of Erickson was his interest in experimenting with people and situations. Not only did he do experiments in the laboratory, but, concerned with laboratory bias, he liked to do them in the field in natural situations. Typically, with whatever group he was with, Erickson might be doing an experiment to see how someone would respond to this or that. He once told me that at a party he might choose someone and apply his "ocular fix" just to see how the person would respond. Or he would set himself the task of having someone move from one chair to another without ever directly asking for that move. Sometimes it seemed to be a way he kept from being bored in situations where his active mind found what was happening to be too routine. At other times he would do more formal experiments in social situations.

I recall an experiment where Erickson said he wished to demonstrate that one could make a person forget something by constantly reminding him of it. Erickson was a master in the control of amnesia and he worked with it in hypnosis as well as in ordinary social relations. The experiment he described was the following. He was teaching a seminar with a group of students at a table. He arranged that a young man who was a chain smoker sit on his right without any cigarettes. While they were discussing the important academic subject of the seminar, Erickson turned to the young man and offered him a cigarette. As the young man reached for the cigarette, Erickson was asked a question by someone on his left. Turning to answer the question, Erickson inadvertently pulled the cigarettes away from the young man before he could take one. The group went on with the discussion and then Erickson seemed to recall that he had been offering a cigarette. He turned, offered one to the young smoker again, and again someone on his left asked him a question, so that he inadvertently pulled the cigarettes away from the young man when he turned to answer it. Of course, the interruptions had been prearranged. All the students except the smoker were aware of the nature of the experiment. After repeating this procedure several times, the young man lost interest in the cigarettes and did not reach out for one when it was offered. At the end of the seminar, the students asked the young man if he had obtained a cigarette. He did not remember having been offered any, having amnesia for what happened. Erickson argued that what was important was the offer and the inadvertent turning away and deprivation. The young man could not blame Erickson for depriving him, because it was clearly not Erickson's fault; yet he was being deprived. This rather classic double bind was responded to by simply forgetting the sequence.

It was constant experimentation of this kind which, I think, gave Erickson not only his wisdom about human behavior but led him to new therapy techniques. For example, Erickson had a procedure for helping a person addicted to medication, such as a tranquilizer. If he refused to give the medication, the person would simply go to another doctor who would provide it. Therefore, Erickson would agree to write a prescription when it was requested, and he would begin to look for a prescription blank among the items on his desk. As he was looking, he would start a conversation with the patient which became increasingly interesting. The conversation would continue until the interview ended. Only after the interview was over would the person realize the prescription had been forgotten. The person would not go to another doctor, because the business with Erickson had not been completed. The person could not blame Erickson for the deprivation, because he was obviously willing to provide but he had *inadvertently* not provided. Just as with the cigarettes, he had benevolently offered it and been distracted. He said the person would begin to lose interest in the medication and forget about it.

Many of us have difficulty adopting Erickson's techniques because of the skill required in carrying them out. The teaching of interpersonal skills has not been part of academic training for a therapist. One of the values of hypnosis is that it teaches one how to give directives. With hypnotic training one learns how to motivate people, how to direct them to behave, how to follow up the response, and so on. This learning is necessary if one does a therapy based upon skill. What set Erickson apart as a hypnotist was his interest and concern with the interpersonal processes of trance induction, not simply the ritual procedure. He argued that a hypnotic induction needed to vary with the type of person the hypnotist was, the nature of the subject, and the particular situation they were in. He liked to see each hypnotic relationship as unique, just as he did with therapy.

The young people here today might find it difficult to realize what it was like to hear Erickson when the ideology of the field was so different. As an example, in the 1950s I was on Gregory Bateson's research project in a Veterans Administration Hospital. I was studying the communication of, and doing therapy with, a 40-year-old man defined as psychotic. He talked, among other things, about how he had cement in his stomach, seeming at times to literally believe that. Constantly he complained about his digestion and this awful feeling in his stomach. At that time the more avant garde of the psychiatric field had made a step forward, or deeper, into the unconscious. From being concerned with the genital stage and the oedipal conflict, the shift in the study of the psychosis had been made to the oral stage. It was a time when the breast was said to be the dream screen and the underlying cause was related to mother's stony breast, which John Rosen talked about, as well as the poison of mother's milk. Being in the avant garde, I was of course interpreting to this poor fellow ideas about his mother and his oral fixation and so on, which I assumed to be the basis of his delusion about having cement in his stomach. The logic of the symbolism was irrefutable.

At about this time I began to talk with Erickson and I asked him what he would do with these delusionary comments of the patient about the cement in his stomach. Erickson said, "I would go with the patient to the hospital dining hall and try out the food." I was astonished at such a shallow approach to this problem. Erickson went on to say that he would teach the patient about digestion, what foods digest easily and quickly, and which digest with difficulty. I felt that Erickson simply did not understand how to approach a psychotic delusion of this kind. It was only some time later that I inadvertently went to the hospital dining hall and discovered the quality of the food. By then I was taking a more practical approach with the patient and even thinking that therapy might do better if he were out of the hospital in the real world rather than sitting on a ward complaining about his stomach.

Several years later, when our project had made great advances, Erickson was still ahead of us. I recall in about 1958 I had been working for some time with psychotics out in the real world in a practical way and we were even doing therapy with the whole family. We had discovered the communication approach and we were clarifying the communication of offspring and parents and bringing out their feelings and ideas about each other. Our goal was to bring about more harmony and closer relationship among the family members. I talked with Erickson at this time about our approach and he said that he thought the attempt to bring about closeness between young adult psychotics and their parents was an error. "This is not a time for closeness," he said, "it is a time when the young person should be disengaging from the family." I felt, of course, that Erickson did not understand the importance of communication theory and was not familiar with the new emphasis on the family that we were developing. It was a few years later that I realized that the problem with a young adult psychotic is not bringing about togetherness with his family but helping parents and offspring disengage and the family survive that change.

I do not wish to imply that Erickson was always ahead of us, or that he always knew and did not himself learn. We too had our influence on him, as I discovered to my surprise one day. In those days Erickson had his own way of doing therapy with a person diagnosed schizophrenic. As an example, he was seeing a woman who was a school teacher and at times she was quite crazy. He persuaded her to keep her delusions locked in the closet of his office where they would be secure and not interfere with her teaching. She did that and saw Erickson irregularly. Then she was going to move to another city and she was worried because she might go mad in that other city and Erickson would not be available. She said she didn't know what to do. Erickson said to her, "If you have a psychotic episode, why not put it in a manila envelope and mail it to me." The woman agreed to do that, and in the other city she continued to function well. Occasionally, she sent Erickson a psychotic episode in a manila envelope. What impressed me with that case was not only that he would think of having the woman put her psychotic episodes in envelopes, but that he saved all those envelopes. He knew that one day she would return and would want to see them. She did just that.

If you examine this therapy, it appears that Erickson was assuming the woman could not be changed but only stabilized. Later, when I was visiting Erickson, he introduced me to a young woman who was showing him her wedding pictures. After she left, he told me that she had been schizophrenic and had made a good recovery. I pointed out that previously he seemed to assume one could only stabilize a schizophrenic, not cure one. I asked him if this was not a change from his past, more traditional view of schizophrenia. He said it was and added, "After all, I've learned something from you people too."

It was Erickson's willingness to change his ways and experiment with new techniques that was his greatest asset. He was a pragmatist. Looking at Erickson and his therapy from the broadest view, it seems apparent in his pragmatism and in other ways that he was very American in his views. The stories and examples he presented were out of life on a farm and

the values of small towns. Whether he was talking of stealing apples from
an orchard, going swimming, or expressing enthusiasm about college life,
his expression seemed to be middle America. He had a basic understanding of growing up in the United States that clarified for him the
stages of family life and the processes of normal living. He knew the
different regions of the country and their particular ideas, styles, and
prejudices. He understood other cultures because he knew this one so well
and could contrast it.

Erickson expressed a different psychiatric tradition from the one with
its roots in Europe, where there was a focus on classification and diagnosis.
Although Erickson was interested in diagnosis, his main interest was in
producing change. He sharply focused on the subject of therapy as an art
in itself, and he emphasized the practical skills needed to carry it out. He
was pragmatic and would shift what he did if it was not working, quickly
adopting some other procedure rather than continue with a failing method
because it was traditional. Not concerned with schools of philosophy,
Erickson focused quite specifically upon the real world and real problems.
He recommended that a therapist use techniques which worked and
discard those which did not, independent of tradition. He did not suggest
you look to a prominent person to lend support to your practices, but
rather that you defend your work by its results. These ideas are considered
characteristic of American pragmatism, just as is Erickson's emphasis
upon taking action rather than being an observer and waiting for change.

In the 1950s there was an explosion of innovative therapies in the
United States. The subject of how to change people came into vogue
rather than a concern with how to study and classify them. The behavioral
therapies developed and so did the family therapies. Everyone became less
philosophical, more pragmatic, and more concerned with social change.
Erickson was premature in the field in that when these changes in therapy
came about he had already changed. One way to describe his contribution
to the present revolution in the field of therapy is to point out that his
position about what to do in therapy was exactly the opposite of what was
done by traditional therapists. It is difficult to believe that he went to such
an opposite extreme from the mainstream of therapy. It is also difficult
to believe that the mainstream of therapy could have been so wrong that
doing the opposite was appropriate. Let me summarize some aspects
of his contribution by contrasting it with the prevailing views of a few
years ago.

HYPNOSIS

In the 1940s and 1950s the field of therapy was largely prevented from using hypnosis. Psychiatrists did not learn hypnosis, and social workers would probably have had their casework buttons torn off if they wanted to hypnotize a client. It was so little taught in clinical training that traveling workshops had to be done to teach it at all. While this condemnation of hypnosis was happening, Erickson was using hypnosis in therapy, developing a wide range of techniques, and advocating that it be a basic skill taught to clinicians.

SYMPTOMS

At that time the field of therapy was not symptom-focused. It was argued that symptoms were unimportant and the real problem was the roots in character structure and personality. As a result, clinicians not only did not know how to change symptoms but argued that one should not. Some vague disaster would occur. Erickson took the opposite position and based his therapy specifically on symptoms. He argued that you change character structure by centering therapy on the specific problem. As he said, the symptom is like the handle of a pot; if you have a good grip on that handle, you can do a lot with the pot. He taught that one should not ignore a symptom but learn all the details about it. As one examined the frequency, intensity, and so on, a proper symptom became something to admire in the way it was involved in all aspects of a person's life. The therapists who ignored symptoms and said one should not deal with them never learned to appreciate the complexity of symptomatic behavior. They also never learned to change what the patient wanted changed.

INSIGHT AND THE UNCONSCIOUS

Erickson deviated most from his colleagues on the issue of insight and the nature of the unconscious. In the 1940s and the 1950s the proponents of insight therapy gained their greatest power. At that time therapists made only interpretations. It was generally assumed that a person's problem was a product of repression and the ideation must be made conscious. Erickson, who had experimented extensively with unconscious repression, slips of the tongue, memories, and dreams, had by the 1940s apparently abandoned that notion as relevant to therapy. It was thought that if a therapist did not bring about insight, he was doing shallow therapy. Erickson took the position that insight therapy did not produce change and even implied that interpretations about internal dynamics could prevent real change.

Erickson's view of the "unconscious" was the opposite of the psychodynamic view of that time. Insight therapy was based upon the idea that the unconscious was a place full of negative forces and ideas which were so unacceptable that they had to be repressed. According to that view, a person needed to watch out for his or her unconscious ideas, and to distrust the hostile and aggressive impulses striving for expression. Erickson took the opposite view and accepted the idea that the unconscious was a positive force which held more wisdom than the "conscious." If a person just let his unconscious operate, it would take care of everything in a positive way. Erickson emphasized trusting one's unconscious and expecting it to fullfill the greatest good. As an example, he said that if he misplaced something and forgot where it was, he did not agitatedly try to find it. He assumed his unconscious had set it aside and would bring it forth at the proper moment.

As a result, you never find in Erickson's therapy statements such as, "Have you noticed that when you mention your husband it is after you mention your father?" or "Have you wondered if you have an unconscious desire to resist this therapy?" He did not assume that insight into unconscious ideas that were repressed was relevant to change. This is why his therapy seemed so strange to an insight therapist. For example, how could such a therapist understand arranging that a depressed woman schedule a certain period of time each week to be depressed? Or how could an insight therapist understand paradoxically encouraging a symptom?

As always, Erickson offered the opposite of insight by encouraging amnesia and changing people outside their awareness. Rather than help patients understand the hidden meaning in dreams or fantasies, he would change them so they dreamed and fantasized differently. He considered an "interpretation" to be an absurd reduction of a complex communication. Similarly, he did therapy with analogies and metaphors differently from the therapists of his time. Erickson was introducing a new theory of change in the ways he used analogical communication. In the past, clinicians worked with the analogies of patients to gain information, as in asking the patient about fantasies and dreams. Or they thought that making the patient aware of the metaphorical meanings in his analogies would cause change, as in discussing the parallels between the content of a fantasy and a real life situation.

Erickson took quite the opposite view; making people aware of the parallels in their analogical presentations would not cause change and would even prevent change. The awareness would reduce the complexity of the issues being changed. If, for example, he was talking about food and eating as a way of influencing a person to have more enjoyment in sex and to be less inhibited, he would be careful not to let the person become conscious of the parallel between eating and sex. As he put it, if they begin to be aware, one should "drift rapidly away from the subject." What he seemed to be suggesting was that therapy done in this way had two requirements: First, one must talk about something that is analogical with something about the patient one wishes to change. That is, one talked about A in order to change B when they had similarities. Once the analogy was being drawn, the therapist also needed to take a position on how A should be in order to change B. Merely talking about A and drawing the analogy was not sufficient, and making the analogy conscious would destroy the change. For example, to talk about eating food as analogic to sex is not sufficient in itself. The therapist must also take a position that food should be enjoyed. For example, he might say there should be pleasure in the appetizers to wake up the gastric juices before the main course. It is saying how something should be when talking about the analogical area that is the cause of change. I think that is what gave Erickson so often the quality of being an ethical lecturer; he emphasized how things should be in one area to change another area.

Consider another example of how Erickson worked outside awareness. If one sees a person caught up in a repeating cycle of behavior with other people, the traditional approach is to make the person aware of the cycle on the assumption that if he becomes aware of it he can stop repeating his behavior. Erickson did not bring about awareness of the cycle but simply set out to change it. He might even induce amnesia for behavior in the cycle so the person would do something and forget he did it. Therefore he would do it again. This repetition would force the other people in the cycle to respond differently and so the repeating pattern would change.

Although Erickson did not offer the usual insight, he was an educator. He would teach patients that life is more complex than they thought by using riddles and puzzles. Often he did explicit teaching about medical and other issues. He was teaching people about their sexual organs and instructing them in specific sexual practices long before "sex therapy" became permissible and fashionable. That too added to the controversy about him.

POSTURE OF THERAPIST

Traditionally, the therapist was an objective consultant to a patient. He or she was an observer who reflected back what was produced and helped the person understand his or her problems and motivation. Rather than intervene into a person's life, the therapist took a position on the outside as a non-participant observer. If asked if his job was to change someone, the therapist would say it was not, it was to help people understand themselves so they could choose to change if they wished. The therapist was not really responsible for change, so if therapy failed it was the patient's fault. Therapists took money from patients to change them, while declining to take responsibility for changing them. A curious paradox of the field.

If we ask what the opposite of the traditional therapeutic posture would be, there we find Erickson. He assumed it was his responsibility to change a patient. If change did not occur, he had failed. I can recall him saying, often in a grim tone, "That case is still defeating me." He was not an objective observer or a consultant; he was an active intervenor into the person's life. He assumed that what he did and said was the cause of change, not some objective awareness that the patient achieved. He would visit the home or office of a patient and escort them to places they feared.

Even psychoanalysts who were thought to be closely involved with their patients thought that Erickson entered too much into a patient's life. I recall Frieda Fromm-Reichmann's comment. She had the reputation of being a therapist most intimate with her patients in intensive therapy. When we said we were studying Erickson, she said, "Couldn't you have chosen a therapist to study who is less involved with his patients?"

Even though Erickson was personal with patients, he was not a pal as many humanistic therapists are. He kept his professional distance while being a friend and confidant. As with many aspects of Erickson, his closeness and distance were paradoxical.

As an example, he was once defining the nature of hypnotic trance as a focusing of attention, and he said amnesia was a product of that attention. He said that he could be talking with a patient about something emotionally moving, and at that point he would kick off his shoes. He would put the shoes on again and later ask the patient about that action. The patient would not remember it happening. Although Erickson was talking about concentration and amnesia, I was thinking about *him*. He could be closely involved enough with the patient to bring out something emotionally moving, and simultaneously he would be distant enough to experiment with kicking off his shoes.

BRIEF THERAPY

At that time it was assumed that long-term therapy was necessary to bring about change. Brief therapy was just a matter of doing less than you did in long-term therapy; you just gave less insight. Erickson worked in quite an opposite way by doing therapy as briefly as possible. When he did long-term therapy, it was when he could not solve the problem more briefly. Instead of seeing someone methodically several times a week, he worked intermittently and for different lengths of time.

Even the way he talked about brief therapy was paradoxical. He said the way to get a quick change was to proceed slowly. He would say, for example, if you get a one-second change in a symptom that exists 24 hours a day, you have made a major change. Often with hypnosis he would increase a one-second change by geometrical progression — from one to two to four and so on. The small change inevitably led to the larger one. As Erickson put it, if you want a large change you should ask for a small one.

Erickson's brief therapy also occurred in the real world. He practiced a therapy of common sense in that he had resources in the community to help his clients, whether it was a hairdresser, a clothing salesman, a waiter in a restaurant, or whatever might be needed. He was familiar with the day-to-day operations of normal living, knew what average families were like, and understood what children did at different stages of development. He was familiar with the problems of growing old and knew intimately the difficulties of dealing with pain and physical illness.

DIRECTIVE THERAPY

Traditionally a therapist was non-directive. It was considered wrong to tell someone what to do, whether in large issues or in what to talk about in the room. There was a naive assumption that one could talk with a patient for months, even years, without directing him in what should be said or done.

Erickson took the opposite position. He argued that change came about by the therapist being directive. He also assumed that whatever one said or did in the presence of a client was directive; the problem was how to do that skillfully rather than assuming it was not happening.

INVOLVING FAMILY MEMBERS

Traditionally, it was not proper to see the relative of a patient; many therapists would not even talk to one on the telephone for fear some terrible damage would be done to the therapy. As always, Erickson, quite the opposite, was willing to see relatives and was one of the earliest therapists to bring family members together in an interview. Sometimes he would see parents and child together, sometimes separately, just as he would see couples both together and individually. He was one of the first to have worked out specific procedures for persuading reluctant relatives to come in when they declined. As an example, when a husband would not come to therapy with his wife, despite an invitation, Erickson would begin to arrange that he come in. Talking to the wife, Erickson would say, "Your husband would probably understand the matter this way," and at another point he would say, "I'm sure your husband would have this view." Each time he would suggest a view or an understanding that was incorrect and not the husband's view. When the wife went home, the husband would interrogate her about the therapy session. She would reveal the misunderstandings of his views that Erickson expressed. Soon the husband would say that he wanted an appointment to "straighten that psychiatrist out," and he would come in.

Erickson was quite comfortable with families. While Freud said he did not know what to do with relatives of patients, Erickson said he did. More than any other therapist of his time, Erickson defined symptoms as contracts between relatives — not merely the expression of an individual. He was also willing to do therapy with friends and colleagues. Not concerned with maintaining a mystical relationship with a patient, he could see a person both professionally and socially.

In summary, traditional therapists were non-directive, consultants to the individual patient. At their most active they encouraged patients to talk and express themselves. They did not use hypnosis, did not give directives, avoided relatives and did not interview families, and did not deal with symptoms. They relied almost entirely on interpretations to cause change in both individual and group therapy.

Erickson developed an opposite approach on each of these variables. He was an active participant in the lives of patients, used hypnosis, gave both paradoxical and straightforward directives, included relatives in therapy, did not make insightful interpretations or do group therapy, encouraged amnesia, and focused specifically on symptoms.

If we look at the multitudinous schools of therapy today and the general trajectory of the field, it would seem that the mainstream has largely swung toward Erickson's position. His approach in therapy is now acceptable and taught, while the position of his opponents is becoming an historical curiosity. If Erickson were 50 years old at this time and at the height of his strength, I think he would dominate the field of therapy. One might think it is sad that he was 20 years ahead of his time and so not fully appreciated when he was in his younger years. However, I think it is better to think about how he helped to create our time. If Erickson had not done his work and taught so widely, we would not have the therapeutic ideas and opportunites we have today.

Choosing any aspect of Erickson and his work to talk about means neglecting some other aspect. The complexity he appreciated in human beings was well expressed in himself. If one emphasized Erickson's concern with people in the real world, one must also recall that he quite fully developed the world of fantasy. To Erickson the human mind was a many-chambered room with entrances and exits which often operated independently of each other. One can have secrets from other people, as well as secrets from oneself. Erickson was as comfortable with the interior of people and their dream states as he was with a child's difficulties with arithmetic in school.

In this presentation I have tried to cover some general and specific issues about Erickson. Doing so, I face Erickson's view that making explicit and conscious any idea about human life reduces a complex subject to an oversimplification. That problem applies to what I have said here about this extraordinary man and his work. In time I think other people will understand him more fully than we do now. Therefore, in closing, let me paraphrase a comment once made by A. N. Whitehead about a speaker. I hope that in this presentation I have left unobscured the vast darkness of the subject of Milton Erickson.

4

A Review of
Ordeal Therapy
(1984)

One day a man, an attorney, came to me for help because he could not sleep at night. His insomnia was beginning to cost him his career because he was falling asleep in the courtroom. Even with heavy medication he was sleeping less than an hour or two each night. I had just begun private practice, and the man was sent to me to be hypnotized to solve his sleep problem. He was not a good hypnotic subject. In fact, he responded to suggestions for hypnosis just as he did when trying to sleep: He would suddenly rouse up wide awake and alert as if frightened by some thought he could not describe. After several tries, I decided hypnosis would not be the way to influence this man's sleeping problem. Yet I felt I had to do something. He'd been through traditional therapy, and nothing had helped him with his problem, which was getting progressively worse to the point that he feared he would become unable to function.

The attorney insisted that nothing was wrong with him or his life; he was happy with his work and with his wife and children. His only problem was that he couldn't sleep. As he put it, "When I start to go to sleep, something pulls me awake, and then I lie there for hours."

Finally, I tried an experiment. I suggested that at bedtime he create a pleasant situation, with his wife bringing him warm milk, as she had before. Then when he lay down to sleep, he must deliberately think of all the most horrible things he might think about or might do or see himself doing. I asked him to practice, in the interview with me, thinking of those awful things, and he couldn't think of any. When I had him think of all the horrible things a hypothetical person, "Mr. Smith," might have on his

61

mind, however, he thought of murder, homosexual acts, and other exciting things like that. I told him that he was to lie down to go to sleep that night, but instead of trying to go to sleep, he should deliberately think of all the horrible things he could bring to mind. As he was leaving the office, he said, "You mean things like putting my wife in a whorehouse?" I said, "That's a good one."

The man went home and followed the instructions. He fell asleep immediately and slept the night through. From that point on, he used that procedure, and he lost his insomnia.

At that time, during the 1950s, there was no therapeutic theory to explain the creation of such an intervention or its success. The only theory was the psychodynamic theory of repression, which would have assumed that telling the man to think awful things would keep the man awake rather than put him to sleep, since it would mean bringing repressed material near consciousness.

At that time there was also no explanation of a rapid therapeutic change because there was no theory of brief therapy. It was assumed that if one did brief therapy, one merely did less than was done in long-term therapy. Therefore, my directive had no rationale. As I puzzled over why that case and similar ones were successful, I decided I should go and consult Milton H. Erickson.

I had learned hypnosis from Dr. Erickson, and had talked with him about hypnosis as part of a research investigation. Finally I had begun teaching classes in hypnosis myself to local physicians and psychologists. When I went into practice as a therapist, I realized at once that hypnosis in research and teaching was not relevant to hypnosis used clinically. I knew how to give people hypnotic experiences, how to provide deep trance phenomena, and how to talk with them in metaphors about their problems. But I really didn't know how to use hypnosis to change anyone.

At that time Milton Erickson was the only consultant available to me who knew something about the use of hypnosis in brief therapy. I was also aware that he had a variety of brief therapy techniques not using hypnosis. These had come up incidentally in conversations about other matters. Actually, he was the only person I knew who was offering anything new in therapeutic technique or theory.

When I consulted with Dr. Erickson, I discovered that he had routine procedures using special ordeals to cause a change and that they were similar to the one I had devised for the attorney. I also found explanations and ways of thinking about other cases that puzzled me. For example, I had been curing a woman's severe headaches by encouraging her to have the headaches as a way to get control of them. As I talked with Erickson, I realized that his therapeutic techniques included paradoxical interventions of just that kind.

Let me present in Dr. Erickson's own words an ordeal procedure for an insomnia case he described to me:

I had a sixty-five-year-old man come to me who had suffered a little insomnia fifteen years previously, and his physician gave him sodium amytal. Three months previously his wife had died, leaving him alone living with his unmarried son. The man had been regularly taking fifteen capsules, three grains each — a dosage of forty-five grains of sodium amytal. He went to bed at eight o'clock, rolled and tossed until midnight, and then he would take his fifteen capsules, forty-five grains, a couple of glasses of water, lie down, and get about an hour and a half to two hours' sleep. Then he would rouse up and roll and toss until getting-up time. The fifteen capsules no longer worked since his wife died. He had gone to the family physician and asked for a prescription for eighteen capsules. The family physician got frightened and apologized for ever allowing him to become a barbiturate addict. He sent him to me.

I asked the old man if he really wanted to get over his insomnia — if he really wanted to get over his drug addiction. He said he did, and he was very honest and very sincere. I told him he could do it easily. In taking his history I had learned that he lived in a large house with hardwood floors. He did most of the cooking and the dishwashing, while the son did the housework — especially the waxing of the floors, which the old man hated. He hated the smell of floor wax, and the son did not mind. So I explained to the old man that I could cure him, that it would cost him at the most eight hours' sleep, and that's all — which would be a small price to pay. Would he willingly give up eight hours' sleep to recover from his insomnia? The old man promised me he would. I told him that it would mean work, and he agreed that he could do the work.

I explained to him that instead of going to bed that night at eight o'clock he was to get out the can of floor wax and some rags. "It will only cost you one hour and a half of sleep, or two hours at the most, and you start polishing those floors. You'll hate it, you'll hate me; you won't think well of me as the hours drag along. But you polish those hardwood floors all night long, and go to your job the next morning at eight o'clock. Stop polishing the floor at seven o'clock, which will give you a whole hour for rising. The next night at eight o'clock, get up and wax the floor. You'll really polish those floors all over again, and you won't like it. But you'll lose at most two hours of sleep. The third night, do the same, and the fourth night, do the same." He polished those floors the first night, the second night, and the third night. The fourth night he said, "I'm so weary following that crazy psychiatrist's orders, but I suppose I might as well." He'd lost six hours of sleep; he had two more to lose before I cured him, really. He said to himself, "I think I'll lie down in bed and rest my eyes for half an hour." He woke up at seven o'clock the next morning. That night he was confronted with a dilemma. Should he go to bed when he still owed me two hours of sleep? He reached a compromise. He'd get ready for bed and get out the floor wax and the polishing rags at eight o'clock. If he could read 8:15 on the clock, he would get up and polish the floors all night.

A year later he told me he had been sleeping every night. In fact, he said, "You know, I don't dare suffer from insomnia. I look at that clock and I say, 'If I'm awake in fifteen minutes, I've got to polish the floors all night, and I mean it, too!'" You know, the old man would do anything to get out of polishing the floors — even sleep.

When Dr. Erickson described that case to me, I realized at once that the procedure I had developed for the attorney was formally the same. I had arranged that the attorney go through an ordeal that he'd rather avoid by sleeping. Dr. Erickson had given his client a task that he'd rather sleep than carry out. Here was a procedure based on a rather simple premise: If one makes it more difficult for a person to have a symptom than to give it up, the person will give up the symptom. Over the years I have made use of this type of intervention in a variety of ways, and in this chapter I will describe the range of variations.

The ordeal process is different from some of the other therapeutic techniques originated by Milton Erickson. His use of metaphor, for example, when he would change "A" by emphasizing "B" in an analogous way, is not an ordeal procedure. In some uses of the metaphoric approach, little is directly asked of the client except to listen. Similarly, Erickson's cumulation of change procedures is quite different from providing an ordeal. A person who is asked to give up pain for a second, and then to increase that to two seconds, and then to four, is going through a geometrical progression toward improvement in which no ordeal seems to be involved.

If we examine Dr. Erickson's innovations in the use of paradox, we can note that he had a person experience a distressing symptom deliberately, and that is not an ordeal procedure. Or is it? Doesn't it fall into the category of giving up a symptom to avoid an ordeal? It appears possible that ordeal therapy is not merely a technique but a theory of change that applies to a variety of supposedly dffferent therapeutic techniques. Before proceeding further with this notion, it might be best to describe the variety of ordeal procedures and their stages.

THE ORDEAL TECHNIQUE

With the ordeal technique, the therapist's task is easily defined: It is to impose an ordeal appropriate to the problem of the person who wants to change, an ordeal more severe than the problem. The main requirement of an ordeal is that it cause distress equal to or greater than that caused by the symptom, just as a punishment should fit the crime. Usually, if an ordeal isn't severe enough to extinguish the symptom, it can be increased in magnitude until it is. It is also best if the ordeal is good for the person. Doing what's good for you is hard for anyone and seems particularly difficult for people who seek therapy. Examples of what's good for people are exercise, improving the mind, eating a healthy diet, and other self-improvement activities. Such ordeals may also include making a sacrifice for others.

The ordeal must have another characteristic: It must be something the person *can* do and something the person cannot legitimately object to. That is, it must be of such a nature that the therapist can easily say, "This won't violate any of your moral standards and is something you *can* do." There is one final characteristic of a therapeutic ordeal: It should not harm the person or anyone else.

Given these characteristics, the ordeal offered might be crude, like a blunt instrument, or ingenious and subtle. It may also be a standard one that can be applied to many problems. Or it may be carefully designed for a particular person or family and not be appropriate for any other. An example of a standard ordeal is to exercise in the middle of the night whenever the symptom has occurred that day. An example of an ordeal designed for a particular person would require too lengthy a description here; readers will find individually tailored examples throughout this chapter.

One final aspect of the ordeal: Sometimes the person must go through it repeatedly to recover from the symptom. At other times the mere threat of an ordeal brings recovery. That is, when the therapist lays out the ordeal as a procedure and the person agrees to experience it, he or she often abandons the symptom before the ordeal even goes into effect.

Types of Ordeals

A few of the different types of ordeals can be listed with examples.

Straightforward task. When the ordeal is a straightforward task, the therapist clarifies the problem and requires that, each time it occurs, the person go through a specific ordeal. During the interview, the therapist finds out, often without making it clear what the purpose is, what the client should do more of that would be good for him or her. A typical response is that the person should do more exercising. The therapist therefore directs the person to go through a set number of exercises each time the symptom occurs. It is often best to have these exercises occur in the middle of the night. That is, the person is asked to go to sleep with the alarm set for three o'clock in the morning and then to get up at three and do the exercising. After that, the person goes back to sleep, so the procedure is like a dream or nightmare. The exercise should be sufficient so it can be felt in the muscles the next day.

As an example, with a man who became anxious when he spoke in public as his job required, I had him exercise each night when he had been more anxious than he thought he should be. The exercise needed to be severe enough so that he could feel it in his muscles at a meeting the next day. He was soon surprisingly calm when he stood up to speak. I learned this from Dr. Erickson who described the procedure in the same type of case with an emphasis on using energy. His patient had a ritualistic, phobic, panicky reaction to his television broad-cast — forced panting, breathing, and for fifteen minutes he would stand gasping, and gasping, and choking, and his heart would pound. Then they would say, "You're on," and he would broadcast over TV with the greatest of ease. But each day he became increas-ingly more miserable. At first it started with a minute or two; by the time he came to see me it was built up to fifteen minutes. He was looking forward to twenty minutes, thirty minutes, an hour; and it was beginning to interfere with his other work at the station. A day after I found out what his sleeping habits were, I gave him that concept of so much energy. As you would expect, his sleeping habits were rather ritualistic. Always in bed at a certain hour. Always up at a certain hour. After I got the concept of energy pounded into his head, I pointed out to him, why not use up that energy that he spent that way? [Demonstrating panting] How many deep squats would it take each day? I told him I didn't know how much energy it would take, but that I thought he ought to start out with twenty-five (in the morning before he went to work), even though I thought at least a hundred would be requisite. But he could start out with twenty-five. . . . No one wants to do that. . . . His lame, sore legs all day long convinced him that he had used up plenty of energy. He had none left over for that [demonstrating panting]. He liked that use of his energy. He built up his knee squats, deep squats, as a health matter to reduce his obesity. Then he began going down to the gym to exercise, and he began to enjoy that daily ritual of going to the gym.

He came back to me and said, "My trouble is recurring. . . I noticed the other day I took three or four deep breaths, and the next program I increased the number, so it is starting to build up. Now what are you going to do? Because doing the exercises won't work. I've got a lot more energy." I said, "It's a profound psychological reaction you're showing." He said, "Yes." I said, "Well, suppose we work on it at the psychological level. Now, I know your sleeping habits. You sign off at ten o'clock. You go right home. You just sum-marize the day to your wife, and then you go right to bed. You sleep eight hours. You're a sound sleeper. You enjoy your sleep, you're a regular sleeper. After four hours' sleep, get up and do a hundred squats." He said, "That I would really hate." I said, "Yes, you can really use up a lot of psychological energy hating that idea. How do you think you'll feel psychologically every night when you set your alarm, as you always do, realizing that you can take up a lot of psychological energy panting in front of the microphone and the television camera? You can take out an awful lot of psychological energy in two ways: . . . setting your alarm for the regular time and psychologically considering with a great deal of intensity of feeling how you don't want to get up in four hours' time to do deep squats."

That analogy worked — for a while. He came back. . . . I said, "So you have got an excess of energy." He said, "That's right." I said, "Now tell me, what has been your lifelong ambition?" He said, "To own my own home for my wife and my child." I said, "It will really make you sweat, won't it, to buy a home and mow the lawn?" He said, "My wife has been after me for years, and I flatly refused to budge, but we're buying one this month." He's had no recurrence. He's got a home. He's got a yard. He's using up all excess energy.

This is not only typical of Dr. Erickson's ordeal therapy but typical of the way he created a therapeutic procedure and then arranged that it be built into the person's natural environment so the influence would continue without therapy.

When a straightforward task is chosen, it can be whatever individual clients say is something they should do more of to improve themselves. A classic approach of Dr. Erickson's with insomnia, for example, was to have the person stay up all night reading those books he or she should have read but had put off reading. Since clients might fall asleep if they sat in a chair to read, Dr. Erickson would require them to stand up at the mantle and read all night long. With such an arrangement, clients either sleep, which is good for them, or read the books they should read, which is good for them. Erickson reports that a person will say, "I'm ready if I ever have the problem again. I've bought a whole set of Dickens." The solution gives clients confidence that they can deal with the problem if it occurs again.

Paradoxical ordeals. The ordeal can be the symptomatic behavior itself and so be paradoxical — defined as encouraging the person to have the problem he or she came to the therapist to recover from. For example, a person wishing to recover from depression can be asked to schedule the depression at a certain time each day. Preferably it should be a time when the person would rather be doing something else. For example, the therapist may schedule someone to concentrate on being depressed at a time when free of other obligations, such as just after putting the children to bed during the time when one might relax and watch television.

It is a question whether a paradoxical intervention can be anything but an ordeal insofar as individuals are asked to go through what they'd rather recover from. An example is the flooding technique in behavior therapy: A person afraid of bugs and wanting to recover from that fear is asked to experience the fear of imagining bugs crawling all over him. This type of paradoxical intervention is obviously an ordeal. Similarly, requiring a quarreling couple to quarrel, or asking a couple to go through a distressing sequence that they wish to stop, is not only paradoxical but an ordeal.

To put this matter another way, insofar as a therapeutic paradox is defined as the person's rebelling against the therapist by not doing the problem behavior, there must be an ordeal involved for the person to resist doing it.

One other relevant aspect of the paradoxical intervention is the way it involves making an involuntary act, which is the definition of a symptom, voluntary. The person must deliberately do that which he or she says can't be helped, such as eat impulsively, or avoid eating, or have aches and pains, or be anxious. When done deliberately, it is, by definition, no longer a symptom. With an ordeal arrangement, one can ask that the person repeat the symptom deliberately each time it occurs involuntarily, thus making the symptom an ordeal for having experienced the symptom. If a person has two symptoms, one can be required each time the other occurs, thereby introducing a paradoxical ordeal that is effective with two symptoms at once. For example, a person who has a particular compulsion and also suffers from extreme shyness can be required to socialize as an ordeal whenever the compulsion occurs.

The therapist as an ordeal. There are several classes of ordeals that are effective because of the effect on the relationship with the therapist. All ordeals are in relation to the therapist and effective because of that, but some are specifically set up to be therapist-oriented.

For example, when a therapist "reframes" an act, the message becomes the ordeal. Any act that is defined in one way by the client can be redefined in a less acceptable way by the therapist so that it is something the person doesn't like. For example, something the client describes as vengeful can be redefined as protective and encouraged by the therapist. Or an act that the client defines as independent of the therapist can be redefined as done for the therapist, thereby reframing it in such a way that the person would rather not continue it.

Another class of ordeals is the confronting techniques used by some therapists. When a therapist forces the client to face what the client would rather not face, and the client has sought out this painful experience, it can be classed as an ordeal procedure. Similarly, insight interpretations that the client doesn't like are an ordeal to experience. In such cases the therapy itself, rather than a specific act by the therapist, becomes an ordeal for a person, and the ordeal must continue as long as the person has the problem.

The fee, or any other benefit to the therapist, can be used as an ordeal by increasing it when the symptom continues or is worse, a type of ordeal some therapists like to impose.

Ordeals involving two or more persons. An ordeal can be designed for one person or for a unit of any size. Milton Erickson had a series of ordeals for children's therapy in which the task was an ordeal for both parent and child. In a typical procedure, for example, a bedwetting child was required, each time his bed was wet in the morning, to practice his handwriting and improve it. His mother was to wake him at dawn each morning, and if his bed was wet, she'd get him up and help him practice his handwriting. If his bed was dry, he didn't have to — but his mother still had to get up at dawn each morning. The procedure became an ordeal for mother and child that resulted in their pride in his giving up bedwetting and improving his handwriting.

With a family, ordeals are possible that can include a couple's burying a past romantic affair by going through a ritual ordeal together that is ostensibly to make the offender suffer but is actually an ordeal for both of them. Or a whole family can be put through an ordeal when a member misbehaves.

These examples indicate a wide range of possibilities; the therapist need only provide something the person would rather give up the symptomatic behavior than do. However, a sharp distinction needs to be made between therapeutic, benevolent ordeals and those ordeals that cause a person to suffer either for the advantage of a therapist or for social control reasons. Simply to lock someone in jail when he or she steals does not fall into the category of ordeal therapy but is a method of social control. All therapists should be on guard against persecution of the public under the guise of therapy. To make it quite clear, the ordeal should be voluntary by the person and good for the person experiencing it but not necessarily for the person imposing it, except insofar as there is satisfaction in successfully helping someone to change when he or she wishes to.

One must always keep clearly in mind the context of any therapeutic intervention. For example, Milton Erickson once devised a procedure in which a boy out of control was sat on by his mother as a way of helping him become less self-destructive. Later this procedure was adopted by inpatient institutions as a way the staff could force children to behave. There is a sharp distinction between a loving mother reforming a child for his benefit under a therapist's guidance and a staff getting revenge on a problem child under the guise of help.

Ordeals, whether in life as a happenstance or in therapy on purpose, do not in themselves have positive effects. Only when ordeals are used with skill are the effects positive, and skill is required in the use of this technique, as in all effective therapy. To use a knife correctly in surgery is rather different from accidentally slashing here and there with a knife while stumbling through an operating room. Similarly, to inadvertently cause a person to suffer is one thing; to arrange it deliberately is quite another.

Stages of Ordeal Therapy

As with any planned therapy, the use of an ordeal should be a step-by-step process with each stage carefully done.

1) The problem must be defined clearly. Since the person has a consequence, an ordeal, whenever the problem occurs, it is best to define the problem clearly. As an example, the person can be asked whether he can tell the difference between normal anxiety and the special anxiety he is coming to therapy to recover from. Everyone is anxious at times in some situations. The distinction must be clear because the ordeal will follow on the presence of abnormal anxiety only. Sometimes that distinction becomes clearer after the ordeal procedure has been suffered and the person is more serious about it. One can also use ordeals for a general feeling of boredom or lack of well-being as a way of driving the person into a more interesting life, but that procedure needs to be carried out with more caution than the more simple ordeal following on a clearly symptomatic act.

2) The person must be committed to getting over the problem. If a person is to go through an ordeal, he or she must really want to get over the problem presented. The motivation to get over it does not always exist at the time of entering therapy. The therapist must help motivate the person to take this kind of drastic step. Offering a benevolent concern, the therapist must bring out of the client a determination to get over the problem. The procedures are similar to getting a person to follow any therapeutic directive, with the additional fact that this type of directive will be unpleasant to follow. Typically the therapist must emphasize the gravity of the problem, outline the failed attempts to get over it, make it a challenge that the client is up to facing, and emphasize that the ordeal is a standard and usually successful procedure.

An important motivation of many clients in this situation is to be willing to go through the ordeal to prove the therapist wrong. Such people have usually tried many things to get over their problem; and if the therapist takes a firm position that this procedure will solve it, the client finds that hard to believe. Yet the only way the client can disprove it is by going through the procedure. Doing that has its therapeutic effect.

One way to motivate a client is to say that there is a cure that is guaranteed, but the client will not be told what it is until he or she agrees in advance to do it. Sometimes clients are asked to come back next week only if they're willing to do whatever is asked. Intrigued at the idea that something can be done to get over the problem, and not believing that, they are placed in a situation where they must agree to do something to find out what that something is. In that way they are committed to do the task.

One should keep in mind that in most cases the ordeal is effective *in relation* to the therapist. It is done to prove the therapist wrong, or else recovery is fast because of the therapist. Typically, for example, if the therapist is asking the person to stay up all night and lose sleep, or get up at night and clean house for an hour, it should be emphasized that the *therapist* is not going through that ordeal. The therapist can say, "I know how hard it is to get up in the middle of the night like that, because I myself so enjoy sleeping soundly all night through." Consequently, when the person is up in the night, he or she is thinking of the therapist enjoying a night's sleep.

3) An ordeal must be selected. The selection of an ordeal is done by the therapist, preferably with the client's collaboration. The ordeal must be severe enough to overcome the symptom, it must be good for the person so that he benefits by doing it, it must be something he can do and will accept in terms of its propriety, and the action must be clear and not ambiguous. It should have a beginning and an end clearly established.

The ordeal procedure is most likely to be followed if the client is involved in selecting the ordeal. Once it is explained to clients that they need to do something voluntarily and then the involuntary reaction of the symptom will cease — or some similar explanation — then they will think of tasks to be done. The therapist must require that the task be good for them so they don't set off punishing themselves in unfortunate ways. If they've designed a positive task themselves, they tend to carry it out with more enthusiasm, and if it's necessary to increase the severity of the task, they respond well.

4) The directive must be given with a rationale. The therapist needs to give the directive clearly and precisely so there is no ambiguity. He or she must make clear that the task is to occur only with symptomatic behavior and that there is a set time for it. Exactly what is to be done must be described. If appropriate, the task must be given with a rationale that makes it seem reasonable. Generally it should be a variation on the theme that if the client does something harder on herself than the symptom, the symptom will disappear. For some people, it is best not to explain but simply to tell them to do it. This more magical approach is best for the intellectuals among the clientele who can undo or explain away any rationale and find the whole thing not necessary.

If the ordeal is at all complex, or if there is a question about its nature, writing it down is helpful to both client and therapist.

5) The ordeal continues until the problem is resolved. The ordeal must be done precisely each time it should be done and must continue until the symptomatic behavior disappears. Typically the contract should be lifelong.

6) *The ordeal is in a social context.* The ordeal is a procedure that forces a change, and there are consequences to that. The therapist needs to be aware that symptoms are a reflection of a confusion in a social organization, usually a family. The existence of a symptom indicates that the hierarchy of an organization is incorrect. Therefore, when a therapist resolves a symptom in this way, he or she is forcing a change in a complex organization that was previously stabilized by the symptom. If, for example, a wife has a symptom that helps maintain her husband in a superior position as the one taking care of her, that changes rapidly when an ordeal requires the wife to abandon the symptom. She and her husband must negotiate a new relationship contract that does not include symptomatic behavior. Similarly, a man who stops drinking excessively must require his family organization to change because it is no longer adaptive to that symptom. It is best for a therapist to understand the function of a symptom in the social organization of the client. If not able to understand it, the therapist must resolve the symptom warily while watching for repercussions and changes.

It is the social changes that often lead the client to a reaction as the behavioral change occurs. Expectably, the client becomes upset, and that upset is a psychological change related to social consequences. When used correctly, an ordeal does not simply change minor behavior, the person restraining himself rather than go through the ordeal. This therapeutic approach can produce basic character changes as part of the disturbing changes that occur in the person's social organization. One sign of a basic change sometimes occurs when the client reports the experience of going out of his mind at the moment of change. Sometimes, just as the ordeal is proving effective, the client will telephone the therapist and say that something strange is happening. The therapist must reassure him that what is occurring is part of the expected change and help him through the reorganization of his life.

To summarize, symptoms have a function in an organization, and it is best if the designed ordeal takes into account the hierarchical situation of the client and his or her family. If, for example, a grandmother is siding with a child against his mother, it might be appropriate to have an ordeal procedure set up between child and grandmother to encourage more distance between them. Or if a father is abdicating his responsibilities in the family, he can become part of the ordeal procedure that would improve his child. Symptoms are adaptive to organizational structures, and with the change in a symptom the organizational structure will change.

Let me give an example that illustrates the procedures in designing an ordeal as well as the need to take the family organization into account when introducing a change. A 16-year-old youth recently out of a mental hospital had the distressing symptom of putting a variety of things up his behind. He would do this in the bathroom, inserting into his anus various vegetables, paper, Kleenex, and so on. He would then leave the bathroom a mess with all this material. His stepmother would have to clean it up, which she did furtively so the other children wouldn't know about his problem.

What ordeal might be appropriate for this unpleasant behavior? Not only should it be something more severe than the problem so he would abandon that behavior, but it should be good for him in some way. More than that, it should involve a change in the structure of his family organization.

What became apparent in a family interview by Margaret Clark, the therapist, was the way the stepmother was burdened by the problem, and the problems of all the children, while the father went about his business. She implied that when he had had several children to take care of after a divorce, he had married her and simply handed the children and their problems over to her. Clearly there was resentment on her part and a strain on the new marriage. The boy's problem became so severe that the parents did not have to deal with the marital issues between them; this appeared to be part of the function of the symptom.

The question was whether to arrange an ordeal with just the boy or to involve his family. It was decided to involve the family, partly because the boy did not seem motivated to get over the problem and partly to make a structural change possible so the symptom would be unnecessary. How to involve the family was the next step. It seemed logical to put the responsibility for an ordeal procedure in the hands of the father, since he should take more responsibility for solving the problem and burden his new wife less. Father and son could experience an ordeal together each time the symptom occurred. The next step was selection of an ordeal appropriate to the symptom.

The procedure decided on was as follows: Each time the boy put material up his behind and messed up the bathroom, the father would be told about it when he came home from work. The father would take the youth out into the backyard and have the young man dig a hole three feet deep and three feet wide. The boy would bury in the hole all the material that he had been messing up the bathroom with and then cover it up. The next time the symptom occurred, the behavior would be repeated, and this would continue forever.

The father methodically followed the procedure with his son, and in a few weeks the symptom stopped. It was not merely that the boy did not do it; he lost enthusiasm for it, as is typical with the use of the correct ordeal. The father, pleased with his success with the boy, began to associate more with him. The wife, pleased with her husband for solving this awful problem, became closer to him, so that the boy's misbehavior to help them became less necessary. There were other problems with this boy and his situation, so that therapy continued, but the particular symptom was promptly ended and remained gone.

This ordeal had the preferred characteristics: It involved and changed the structure of organization in the family by getting an irresponsible father involved. It was more severe than the symptom, since digging a deep hole in hard ground in the fall in the cold is not a simple task. The father had to stand in the cold with the boy until the task was done, so that his attitude toward a repetition of the symptom became more negative. The boy got exercise, which he wanted, in digging the hole. Digging the hole could be considered metaphoric, as well as paradoxical, to the symptom: He had been putting things in a hole, and he was required by the therapist to put things in a hole. So the procedure involved not only an ordeal but a metaphor, a paradox, and a family organizational change. As with most therapeutic procedures, the more an ordeal deals with various aspects of a situation, the better.

THE ORDEAL AS A THEORY OF CHANGE

Up to this point the ordeal procedure has been discussed as a therapeutic technique that can be considered one of many possible types of intervention to bring about change. If we examine the ordeal in a broader context, it appears to be more than a technique — it is actually a theory of change that encompasses many therapy techniques. Is it possible to say that all types of therapy are effective because an ordeal is explicitly or implicitly involved?

Examining other theories of change, one finds there are really not many contenders on the market. There is the insight theory in its different variations. This is based on the view that men and women are rational, and if they understand themselves, they will change. The schools of therapy based on this premise range from those that probe into unconscious processes through those that offer a rational consideration of alternatives to education of parents in dealing with problem children. Included in this school are the "emotional expression" theories, also based on the theory of repression, the central idea of this theory. Just as insight into repressed unconscious ideas is said to bring about change, so is the expression of repressed dynamic emotions, whether through insight or through primal screaming. The resistances must be "worked through" by discovering ideas and expressing buried emotions.

A second theory of change derives from learning theory and proposes that people change when the reinforcements that determine their behavior are changed. The procedures range from increasing positive reinforcements to replacing anxiety with relaxation to forcing people to change with "aversive" techniques.

A third, increasingly popular theory of change is the idea that people are participants in a homeostatic system and the governors of that system must be reset to bring about change. When reset, either by amplifying a small change or by disorganizing the system and forcing a new system, the problem behaviors of the participants will change. Most of the marital and family therapies flourish within the idea of the systems theory of change.

Theories of change of this kind have several characteristics. First of all, they can explain almost any outcome in any kind of therapy, even those of opposing theories. Enthusiastic advocates will say that the "real" cause of change is based on their theory. So an insight theorist will argue that people experiencing behavior modification procedures changed because they "really" discovered things about themselves during the experience. Similarly, the learning theorist argues that the insight schools of therapy actually change their clients' reinforcement schedules, and that is what "really" produces the change. In the same way, systems theory is broad enough so that its adherents can argue that any method of therapy "really" alters the sequences in a social system and so changes the people involved. Even the entrance of a therapist into a social system must change the sequences.

Another characteristic of theories of change is that they must be conceptualized in such a way that they cannot be disproved. It is the theory no one can disprove, like the theory of the existence of God, which has a fair chance of living forever, if there is money in it.

Can the ordeal as a theory of change meet the challenge of the other theories? Certainly it fits the criterion that it cannot be disproved. One can always argue that all people in therapy go through an ordeal. Even the most ingenious experimentalist could not set up a way of disproving the notion that any therapy is an ordeal. The mere fact that one must ask for help in order to begin therapy is an ordeal. It means that one has failed to solve one's problems and must concede that one needs help. Those who do not ask for help, but enter therapy involuntarily, demonstrate the point even more; it is an ordeal to be forced to go through therapy (and even to have to pay for what one does not want).

Once in therapy, the experience is hardly a rose garden. In the insight therapies one has the unpleasant experience of having all the unfortunate thoughts and deficiencies that one doesn't like to mention examined and dwelt on. If the person objects, the therapist is likely to argue that resistance, and working through that resistance, is expected. One must suffer the exploration of what one would rather not think about. Interpretations are always about what one is reluctant to admit. At a more elementary level, Freud (who knew an ordeal when he saw one) suggested that the fee should be a sacrifice to benefit the analysis, which is an unconscious recognition of the ordeal as the basis of analysis. Whether we examine psychodynamic orthodoxy or one of the spin-off confrontation groups where people face their innermost awfulness, the insight school clearly is based on the premise that an ordeal is basic to change.

Behavior modifiers don't force people to think about their more unpleasant thoughts; they emphasize the more positive side of reinforcements. However, the therapy experience itself often includes the tedium of being lectured on learning theory as well as having someone behave in a programmed way in response to one's intimate distress. The inhuman response to a human dilemma can be an ordeal. Of course, behavior modification also revels in aversive techniques involving explicit ordeals, such as shocking people by word or electricity when they manifest symptoms. Even apparently benign techniques that don't seem aversive, such as Joseph Wolpe's reciprocal inhibition procedure, in which clients imagine their phobic situations, are not cheerful moments. It is unpleasant and can be tedious to go through imagined scene after imagined scene of situations one fears and would rather not think about, and to pay money to do that.

Family therapy also offers ordeals, both intentional and inadvertent. To have to come together with one's family in the presence of an expert and concede that one is a failure as a parent or a child or a spouse is an ordeal. Exploring how one participated in producing a defective member, or even acknowledging that one did so, is ordealful. Therapists using acceptance techniques are likely to advise the family to continue in their misery, as is characteristic of the Milan group. Other therapists use experiential and confronting techniques, offering unpleasant insightful interpretations to the family, thereby causing a family to hint they would rather be elsewhere. Therapists who like to have families weep together and express emotions must focus on bringing out their misery.

Obviously, a sound argument can be made for the ordeal as the "real" cause of change in all contemporary therapy, whatever theories the therapists think they are following. Should we confine ourselves to therapy schools? What about other aspects of human life? One thinks of religion at once. Is not the ordeal the basic rock on which is built the Christian church? Change, or conversion, in Christianity was obviously not based on the idea that the soul is saved through wine and good cheer; rather, salvation comes through misery and suffering. It is when the Christian gives up the pleasures of sex and the grape and accepts the hair shirt that conversion has taken place. The benefits of distress are part of the basic, and curious, concept of salvation through suffering. Everywhere one turns in Christian edifices, one sees the sufferer going through his ordeal on the cross. Turning to specific procedures, in the oldest tradition of the oldest Christian church is confession — an ordeal in which one must, for the good of one's soul, reveal to another that which one would rather not. Equally old in tradition is penance, a consequence of confession. Obviously, penance is a ritualized ordeal. Like therapy ordeals, penance takes two forms — penance as a standardized task and penance designed for the peculiar sins of a particular sinner.

In passing, it might be mentioned that not only Christianity and the Western world have found their way to the ordeal. If we glance at the Eastern philosophies and religions, we see that misfortune is part of enlightenment. Not only are there Eastern religions that emphasize accepting suffering as beneficial, but Zen Buddhism, with its 700-year-old procedures for changing people, includes specific ordeals. The Zen master is likely to bring about enlightenment by striking students with sticks and requiring them to respond to impossible koans. Enlightenment, like salvation and therapeutic change, has painful steps on the way to bliss.

The other area of human life besides religion where change takes place is in the political arena. Here we also find the ordeal. The great revolutionary movements, such as the Communist and Socialist movements, set out to change the masses of the world. To achieve this change, participants in the movement are expected to make sacrifices and go through disciplined ordeals. Every mass movement requires sacrifices and giving up the world of pleasure for the cause. It seems evident that if an individual, or a whole society, is asked to change, the ordeal is central to the process of transformation.

Whether we examine the ordeal as a technique or as a universal theory of change, its merits demand further examination and exploration. As a subject of research and training for many years to come, it has one aspect that needs great emphasis. Like any powerful means of changing people, the ordeal is a procedure that can cause harm in the hands of the ignorant and irresponsible who rush off to make people suffer. More than any other technique, it can be misused by the naive and incompetent. We should all keep in mind that society grants permission to therapists to impose their help on people to relieve suffering, not to create it.

5

Remembering Erickson: A Dialogue Between Jay Haley and John Weakland
(1985)

The following is a transcript of a videotape produced by Jay Haley and donated to The Erickson Foundation. It was shown at an Ericksonian Congress media program.

H: What's your first memory of meeting Milton Erickson?

W: My recollection is that you met him before I did. You went to a workshop and that got the whole thing started. I did not actually meet him until we went to Phoenix for the first time.

H: You met him in Phoenix then?

W: I believe so.

H: I recall that I wanted to take a seminar on hypnosis to study hypnotic communication as part of the Bateson project. I heard that a traveling seminar was coming to San Francisco. So I asked Gregory if I could go up there and learn some hypnosis. He asked who was giving it and I said Milton Erickson. He said, "I will call him," and that way I found out that he knew Milton Erickson; he and Margaret Mead had consulted with him years before.

W: Somehow Bateson knew almost everybody. But you didn't know he knew Erickson.

H: So he called Milton on the phone and said could an assistant of his come up and take the seminar. Milton said yes.

I took that seminar. It was one of those where they lectured and talked, then demonstrated, and then you worked with fellow students to learn how to do it.

Well, one of the things that I remember about that is Erickson talking to the group and then wanting to demonstrate. So he said, "Someone in this group would like to come up and volunteer to be a subject." And the muscle in my thigh just twisted. It was the most curious feeling—an involuntary movement. It almost pulled me up. Then the guy in front of me stood up and went up. So I didn't do anything, but I had never had a feeling like that before.

W: If that guy hadn't stood up reasonably fast, you might have been up on the stage then.

H: That's right. It was a curious feeling. So then I came back and decided to make hypnosis a part of the project. And then we started going to visit Milton and we managed a week a year at least. I think that 1955 was the first visit. My last one was 1971, I believe.

W: You kept going a good deal longer after I stopped.

H: Sixteen or 17 years. Also, whenever he came to Palo Alto, he would call me up and I would go to his seminar.

W: You asked about my memory of my first meeting. I have a memory but I am not sure that it was the first meeting. We went into his house and he was sitting there at his desk and leaning forward and saying, "All right. What is it that you want from me?"

H: I remember once after I went into practice and I went up to talk with him about how to cure people, that was the first line he gave me, "What is it you really want from me?"

I remember his house so well. It was a little brick house, near downtown Phoenix, with three bedrooms, and there were six or eight kids in there.

W: Very modest little place.

H: Yes. And people flying in from New York and Mexico and from all over the world. His living room was the waiting room. The little kids were playing in the living room while the patients were waiting.

W: I remember how very striking that seemed to me then. I had been in more or less analytic treatment in New York where you came in and there was never anyone in the waiting room and you went out through a different door so that you never saw any other patients. And to think that his kids were in there playing with his patients, some of whom he described as really rather far-out people. It was a revelation to me.

H: I remember his wife, Betty, saying to me once that a guy said to her, "Well, I never dressed a doll before." It was Kristi or Roxie who had asked him to dress a doll.

He had a living room and a dining room and on the dining room table was all the stuff from the journal that he and his wife were editing. And then he had this little office which was about 8 × 8, or 10 × 10 at the most, with two or three chairs, his desk and some bookcases.

W: I remember that with just the two of us in there, it seemed to me to be rather full.

H: He liked to have people close enough so that he could reach them, is what he said. He could reach out and take a hand and touch them. In those conversations with him, with the air conditioner going, the dog barking outside, and his wife hollering for the children — it made quite a background. And that clock ticked, ticked, ticked over the desk.

W: All of that, in his way, was characteristic. He didn't think that you had to get in a sanitized soundproof environment to do your treatment, for hypnosis or anything else.

H: One of the things about our visits was that we stayed at a hotel downtown and then we would go spend an hour with him between patients. Then we would go back to the hotel, figure out what he had been saying, revise our plans on what we would ask, and then go back and spend another hour with him, and that was how we would spend the week.

W: Well, we were always making plans and always revising the plans because he never exactly followed our plans.

H: He would tend to tell us what he thought was good for us rather than what we had in mind.

W: It usually had some relation to our questions and our plan, but it was not what you would call a direct answer.

H: He had a style of talking so that you could never be quite sure whether he was talking about you personally, whether he was telling you about a case because it interested him, or whether he was educating you about the nature of the event. All three at once, really. He told us some great cases.

Thinking of that, I was listening to a tape of ours a while back and I heard the first mention of an ordeal therapy, I think. We both thought it was funny and apparently had not heard it before. There was a man who panicked when he had to go up to a microphone in a TV studio. He was a TV announcer. He spent about fifteen minutes gasping for breath, and then he had to go up and talk. Erickson gave him a theory about energy, and excess energy, and had him do deep knee bends every time he was anxious. Then he had him get up in the middle of the night and do deep knee bends when he was anxious. We thought that was hilarious. After that, I tried that in practice with a number of cases and it was very effective. But I think that was the first mention of it and he mentioned it so casually—not like this was an old procedure that he had worked up.

W: I don't remember that that was the first ordeal thing that we heard about. I would have thought it was about having an insomniac get up in the middle of the night and clean the house.

I remember when I heard that, like many things I heard from Milton, I did a funny sort of double take. On the one hand, I thought this is highly interesting and there must be somthing there. It certainly seemed to me that there was, but I couldn't figure out what the devil it was because this was so different from all the treatment that I had ever heard of before.

H: That's the important thing to me—what a contrast he was to everything else that we knew about. At that time we were studying therapy from a number of other people, doing a lot of reading on it, trying to examine the nature of it, and his was so unusual that it was just hard to grasp. It is hard to believe now, because many of these things now seem obvious. But at that time. . . . And to hear those tapes and to hear us laughing every once in a while at something he did that now seems rather routine. . . .

W: I think that there are probably still times when I read about or hear about some of his cases when I get the feeling that there is something that I am grasping that I hadn't grasped before.

H: There were so many things he mentioned that he would expand on if you asked him about them. If you didn't ask, he wouldn't mention it. I don't know if I ever told you this one. We may not have discussed it. Remember that case of the couple who both wet the bed and found each other and got married, and then wet the bed jointly? He had them kneel on the bed, and deliberately wet the bed, and lie down in that wet bed for about 30 days. One time, for some reason, just in passing, I said, "Why kneel?" And he said, "Well, they are religious people. They knelt by the bed every night and prayed anyhow." Now, even that was planned. He could have had them stand on the bed or it could have been done in a different way.

W: Well, I think similarly about the story of the woman he had sit on her obstreperous kid. It wasn't until I had heard that from him the second or third time that it became clear that the woman also had a weight problem and that the intervention was, in addition to everything else, a way of saying, "Your heavy weight can also be constructive."

H: It would make a positive thing out of the negative.

W: And I had not seen that point in it the first time or two at all.

H: It is so rich the way he worked, each detail becomes so important — if you go into it. If you don't go into it, you don't even know it is important.

At the Bateson project we were interested in the parallels between schizophrenia and hypnosis. Since schizophrenics have many characteristics of hypnotic subjects, we were interested if one could induce hypnosis and schizophrenia in the same way. Were they similar? We were first investigating hypnosis with him and then we began to realize that he had a whole new school of therapy that we didn't know about and that's when we got into what he was doing in therapy.

I can recall that when I started a private practice as a hypnotherapist, you and I had been teaching classes.

W: Yes, and over a long period there, holding meetings to practice hypnosis.

H: I learned quite a bit about how to hypnotize people but when I sat down to cure them, that was a different matter. That was a different kind of hypnosis, and I went to ask him about that.

W: Well, that's when that old difficult question comes up, "Now that you are in a trance, what do you do?"

H: The fact that research hypnosis and clinical hypnosis are not necessarily related at all I hadn't thought through until that moment. He used to have hypnotic evenings in Phoenix every week.

W: Yes. I went to at least one of them.

H: I remember that is where we recorded Ruth.

W: That's right. The one we asked about in detail to make that paper of the trance induction and commentary.

H: I think that was the first paper, certainly on hypnosis, in which some-body is asked step by step what they did all the way through it. Since then, it has been done on therapy too. That was the first though. He kept surprising us with what he was doing. What we thought he was doing was somewhat different.

Do you remember the most unusual case you ever heard him talk about then? I remember one he had who was psychotic. She was a schoolteacher with young men floating over her head. And he had her put those young men in the closet in his office so they wouldn't interfere with her school teaching. And then when she was going to leave the city, she said, "What if I have psychotic episodes in the other city?" And he said, "Why don't you put them in a manila envelope and send them to me." And so she sent him her psychotic episodes in a manila envelope. I think that was one of the most extraordinary cases I ever heard from him.

W: Which he finally filed away in the closet.

H: He filed it away. He knew that she would come back and check if he had them. And he saved all of them. He had a drawer full of them. In fact, I remember him pulling open the drawer and there was a whole bunch of manila envelopes in that drawer.

W: Well, that one would be hard to top.

H: It was an extraordinary case — and the quickness of his thinking, and how he related ideas. Putting the young men in the closet led logically to putting the psychotic episodes into the envelope. It was putting something in something.

W: Just filing it away where it wouldn't get in your way.

H: I think she was also the woman who said there was a giant bear trap in the middle of the floor. And he very carefully walked around that whenever she was in the room. He was so courteous to patients.

I have been teaching his therapy as "courtesy therapy," as a way of accepting and joining people and helping them without making a confrontation out of it.

W: Well, it sure fits with that emphasis which I see more of with every passing year. Accept what your client offers you. Don't get in an argument about it. Accept it.

Do you remember, much later, the time he came to MRI and was doing a hypnotic demonstration with a young woman? Her boyfriend heard about it and arrived outside the door boiling mad.

H: I don't remember.

W: I think that was while you were still there. He did a beautiful piece of accepting and it had one of the most dramatic rapid change effects I ever saw. It was all very simple. As he finished the demonstration, he was told the young man was being kept outside. They weren't going to let him into the demonstration. But he was very mad and he wanted to know what they were doing with his girl in there.

Erickson said, "Open the door." As the young man came rushing in, Erickson turned to him and said, "I am very happy to meet you and to find that there is still at least one young man in the world who is concerned to protect his young lady and be sure that she comes to no harm."

All the anger was dissipated because Erickson made no argument about it. "This is wonderful. So pleased to see it." But, how many would do it that way?

H: He was so quick. I remember a time — I think we were both there — a woman and her mother just came and knocked at the door. It turned out that it was a woman who had been in the state hospital and he helped her get out years before. She came to see him. Just dropped in. So he came out and talked to her a few minutes and asked his wife to get a picture. And he gave the girl a picture. She was a Mexican girl. And she was so happy to get that picture. He knew exactly that he should do that. Then he wrote something on it and gave it to her. She expressed her appreciation for his getting her out of the hospital and all, and then she went away.

Later on, in passing, he said, "Did you notice whether I signed that picture on the front or the back?" We had no idea. He said, "Well, the back, of course. I made that decision very quickly because she is going to frame that picture, and then she will discover at that time that this is a personal message to her that no one else can see because it is on the back of the picture."

Now, something like that happened so fast. He had two or three minutes with that woman, and he made a decision that fast. He knew he should give her a picture, that she would be pleased and it would help sustain her. He knew he should put a message on it and it really should be a personal one, not on the front where everybody could see it.

W: The front was for the world and the back is her private and personal information.

H: And he did that so quickly. He was one of the few psychiatrists around who covered the whole range of patients. He was as comfortable with a raving psychotic as he was with a little kid with whom he was playing jacks. He had a tremendous range.

W: I think part of it was that he had seen so much that he was in danger of "I'm going to get bored if I don't see something further, if I don't see the whole range, if I don't try to handle an old problem in a new way."

H: He would do a home visit, which other people would not do at that time. He would take somebody to a restaurant, as well as work in the office. That isn't so uncommon today, perhaps, but in the 50s it was extraordinary for someone to cover that range and to do work outside the office.

W: Well, I think at that time there were a great many people — in fact, probably almost everybody else in the field — who were bound by a multitude of restrictions that they didn't even recognize as restrictions. And one of the things about Erickson in both his life and his practice was he was always getting rid of other people's limits and going beyond them.

H: Beyond his own.

W: Sure.

H: He had a way of making each case a unique approach. One of the things that he was so quick at was just observing people and diagnosing them. I was listening to a tape recently and finding out that in medical school, while he was getting a masters in psychology, he tested just about every mental patient in Wisconsin and just about every criminal in Wisconsin. He tested hundreds of people. So he covered so many kinds of people. He did this deliberately so he would learn about psychopathology of all kinds and meet a broad spectrum of it, while also making a living.

But a lot of people who are so casual about taking up one of his techniques don't realize what a tremendously disciplined gathering of information about people he did for so many years before he sat down with somebody and then quickly did something.

W: Well, yes, I think that they tend to look on Erickson as a magic worker, but this is absolutely antithetical to the way he worked. Because he worked with a great deal of skill, care, and calculation. The magic was only in that the art was concealed.

H: And he was so impatient with students who wanted to do things quickly before they understood the situation. This whole magic hoax stuff around him where he "laid on his hands" and people did things was not really what he had in mind at all about the nature of therapy. You really had to know your business.

W: I have often wondered, and your mention of all this testing brings it up, how he ever found the time to do all the things he did, because he did a lot of things all his life like that.

H: And he spent hours over some automatic writing or something like that.

The thing about him is that in his own life he was as clever as he was with his patients. For example, there was the way he handled the criminal situation. He got interested in medical school or internship—somewhere there—in criminology. He did his first paper on criminology, I believe. And the way he got a job in that was he started to provide, on the desk of the big wheel in the criminal division in Wisconsin, a report of all the crimes committed that week. Something like that. Some statistical report on crime which interested Erickson. And he would put it on the desk of this guy every Monday morning. One Monday morning he didn't do it and the guy sent for him and said, "I want to speak to that man Erickson." He said, "Erickson, you are going to get fired if you don't put this on my desk the way you have been." Erickson said, "Well, you never hired me." And that's how he got the job. It was first making himself valuable and then not doing it so the guy realized that he was valuable and hired him. And that is how he helped pay his way through school. He did so many things like that.

He had such an ability to combine several things at once. Like the fact he mentioned in passing once that a doctor had told him to live in Phoenix for his allergies, but to get out regularly. So he lived in Phoenix but he did traveling seminars regularly. That was part of his professional life and was also for his health.

W: Well, that may be part of the answer to my question of how he did so much. He made combinations so that he was always doing more than one thing at the same time.

H: He also worked very hard. He used to work from seven in the morning to eleven at night, he would see patients and then he left weekends open for people who traveled long distances to spend two or three hours with him.

W: You asked about the most amazing case. This isn't the most amazing but it was one of the most puzzling to me when he first told it to me. I think that I have got some grip on what he was doing now. But when he first told me the case, I kept thinking, What is that about? What is he doing there?

A musician came to him from New York. He said, "I am just so anxious that I can't perform." Milton spent nearly two days of the weekend with him. He spent almost all of the time giving him long dissertations about the need to be flexible, I believe. Long, long stories about how you need to be flexible in various tasks such as typing. I kept thinking, "What is the treatment here?" He had been getting the guy madder and madder at these long boring dissertations. Then, finally, just before he finished, and just before the guy had to catch a plane back to New York, so that he wouldn't have any time to raise any questions, he said, "And if you, with all your experience and training, can't walk up to the platform and play a piece, that wouldn't be very flexible, would it?" And I was flabbergasted. That was another one of those things where. . .there is something very important here, but I can't quite get a hold of it.

H: You know, there was another piece on that one. He first explained to the guy that he himself was tone deaf. Then Milton said, "Let me explain to you how you should play the piano. You should hit the keys with the little finger a little harder than with the forefinger because the little finger is not as strong as the forefinger." And for a concert pianist to listen to Milton who was tone deaf explain how to play the piano. . . .

W: But that was the whole thing, he was building up. . .

H: That guy—by God, had to prove to him that he could. . .

W: That's right. He was building up the motivation of resentment until that guy wouldn't sit still for that final remark.

H: The only way he could prove Erickson wrong was to perform well. Absolutely.

W: But I think part of the difficulty was at that time, like everybody else, I was thinking, Well, there are good motives and bad motives and therapists work with good motives and therapists themselves are full of good motives—like you understand and sympathize with some-body's difficulties. And in that context, you couldn't understand Erickson's treatment.

H: The guy couldn't disagree with him. Everything he said was true and said benevolently and kindly.

W: With a twist to it.

H: I remember him once saying that you had a much greater chance of success with somebody who flew 3,000 miles to see you because they had so much invested in just coming there that they almost had to get over something, because they had put so much into it.

There was another thing that he told us—and this was typical of the way he put it. He said, "I am waiting for a woman to come into my office who has had a very important premarital affair or is having a very important extramarital affair who doesn't tell me that by the way that she sits down in the chair." And the way that he put it was not that women always told that. Rather, he said, "I am waiting for the exception, because they always tell me by the way they sit down in a chair."

He was always interested in the exception. You remember the time he had us come into the office—we were in the living room and he told us to come into the office—and we came in and this girl was sitting in the chair and we looked at her and he sent us out again. Then after she left, he sat us down and said, "What did you see?" Do you remember that?

W: Yes, I remember it, a little vaguely. I don't remember what I saw and what I didn't see, though.

H: I remember that we said, "Well, she was a woman." And we said she was in a trance. And he said, "Well, that's true." And finally he told us that we should have observed that the right side of her face was a little larger than the left side. That the right hand was a little larger than the left. She had some neurological problem. It was evident to him and we were expected to see, and we failed the test.

That was part of the way that he set us up, by asking it in such a general way, "Didn't you see. . . ?" that we didn't know whether he was talking about the hypnosis, trance, this woman, the nature of life, or what. But we sure didn't do well.

W: I think in all probability it was rather deliberate that he didn't give us much hint and it was rather deliberate that he made us fail because in some way, I am sure, he thought that would be instructive and useful for us.

H: That we would do better the next time. We would observe the next time.

I talked to residents whom he had trained and he would give them hell if they didn't do a proper diagnosis. The next time they would observe the patient. I remember that. He was great on observation.

One of the interesting things that was hard for us to grasp in those days, I think, was that he took the way a patient sat down and the way that a patient moved as a message to him. Not just as an expression about the person; he took it that they were telling him something.

It was Gregory Bateson's old notion that such nonverbal behavior wasn't just a report about their nature, it was a command of some kind. And that was hard to see. He was so interpersonal in that sense. He took whatever they did with him as a message. And we took it as, "Well, that's an interesting person," or something like that.

W: We were the ones who were supposed to be interactional.

H: That is true.

And we had many arguments with him about whether something was interpersonal or not. But on that kind of a level he was absolutely interpersonal.

We used to argue with him about a wife's symptom — whether that was an adaptation to a husband who had the same or similar problem. And he often, at least in the early days, in the early 60s, described it like an independent phenomenon while treating it as if it wasn't. That was what was also throwing us. His therapy was absolutely interpersonal while his theory was not.

W: He had the capacity to stick very tight to a view of his, if you called it into question or even wanted to discuss it. That was true when we brought down those ideas about similarities between schizophrenic behavior and trance behavior. He stood quite firm, as I remember, as he did in something I brought up with him many years later.

After reading some of Carlos Castaneda's stuff, I wrote to Milton and said, "I am wondering if Castaneda ever met you because there seemed to be some things about the figure Don Juan that are reminiscent." And he sent me back a rather irritated message: "Absolutely no, and there is no such connection."

H: So many people now think of Erickson as a cult figure and a guru, partly because of the bad shape he was in in his old age. When we knew him, he was young and vigorous and placed a big emphasis on how you should control your voice, you should control your speech, control your body movement, and use all of that in therapy. And what was so sad to me was how he lost control of his speech and movement as he got older. It was really a shame.

I remember once saying to him that I would like to film him. I wanted to set up a camera in his office. He said he would rather not, because he didn't want to be remembered as an old man who couldn't speak well and do his therapy well. Then he let himself be videotaped and now what people have is him as an old man, which is a shame.

W: Well, fortunately, there is still a little around from the earlier period.

H: It was also fortunate that he was able to work as well as he did, given all those handicaps. The people who came back said it was extraordinary what he went through.

W: Well, in a sense, it is the epitomization of his whole career. He was always a man who did his thing in spite of so many handicaps.

H: His whole life. And he loved to tell a story by saying, "I had this impossible situation."

W: Yes. After that, you knew what was coming: "Here is how I did the impossible."

H: It was the way that he liked to present a case. He would lay it on as so impossible and then he would have it all solved. The solutions were usually so obvious once he did it.

Remember that case of inhibited Ann that he told us about? She was the one who had the choking and gasping and it came on just before bedtime. So he talked to her about all the things in the bedroom — the dresser and the drapes. And then he said, "Of course, there is a carpet." I said to him, "You haven't mentioned the bed." And he said, "When I said, 'Of course, there is a carpet,' that bed is mentioned. When you say, 'Of course, there is a carpet,' you are mentioning a bed by not mentioning it." That again was so obvious once he said it, but it wasn't obvious at the time.

W: Well, again, if you make too much of a point of something, it is easier to resist it. And as he comes all around, it comes to mind in a way you can't resist because he is not pushing anything on you.

H: He had this way of getting your participation in hypnosis by partially saying something so you had to finish it. When you finished it, you were participating. Or if you do something incomplete, the other person has to complete it.

*W:*You always pay more attention to what you say yourself than to what somebody says to you. So he gets it started off and you complete the message; therefore, you have told yourself. And you have got to take that seriously.

H: There is a film of him hypnotizing five women in 1964. There is a piece of that we should look at, because if I am right about what he did—and I talked to him later about it and I believe he agreed—it is the most interpersonal piece of hypnosis that I have seen. He said to this woman, "My name is Milton. My mother gave me that name. It is an easy name to write."

As I watched that film, what seemed evident was that he was acting very young. One of the things that he used to say about regressing somebody was that when he regressed somebody back to childhood, he wasn't there. They would have to make him somebody, like a teacher. I think what he was doing with this woman was that if he were childlike, she actually had to become childlike to join him. The way he got her to regress was by regressing himself. And I don't think you could have anything more interpersonal than that in that style of working.

W: I have often found that some of those things he did that looked most simple were the things that you would have to look at hardest to see what the point was.

H: He must have told us hundreds of cases over the years as a way of educating us to get us to think "as simple" as he did about these things.

W: Well, he would have an incredible amount of case material in his head that he could reel off.

H: He would associate to a case as he was talking about it. He had so many cases. The observation and his diagnosis were very complex. It's the interventions that are simple.

W: I think they got more and more so.

H: I think that as he got older, they got more economical. The efficiency with which he worked got better.

I think he got more confronting as he got older, and I think that makes people feel he was more a confronting therapist than he really was in our day. I think perhaps he confronted more when he had fewer skills of physical control. Because we really remember him as a very accepting and joining sort of a therapist, and I think a lot of people don't think of him in that way.

W: I certainly remember him in the early days as someone who was accepting. Also, at the same time, as someone you could readily be fearful of because it was easy to see he was powerful and penetrating even while being accepting. You could shake a little about it as a client.

H: As a client and as a colleague. I think his colleagues were largely afraid of him.

W: I think a lot of them were.

H: Because he did have such a reputation for indirect influence.

W: It wasn't only Gregory who was worried about, "He's invited me to dinner."

H: They were pleased if he was benevolent but a little uncertain that he was.

I don't know if I ever told you about the guy who came to Palo Alto. A man came to see me and asked if I would treat his daughter. I said, "What's the problem?" He said she wasn't doing well. She was depressed or something. He said, "I have been to see Milton Erickson with my other daughter and she is fine." The guy was a wealthy man. So I said, "Why don't you take this daughter to Milton?" And he said, "I am afraid to." And I said, "Why are you afraid to?" He said, "Well, when I took my other daughter there, Dr. Erickson put me under house arrest in Phoenix for six months." And he said, "I don't want to go down there and spend six months again." So I said, "Well, you might not have to this time." And I persuaded him to take the other daughter down. He did, and Erickson didn't put him under house arrest. That was a family that Erickson stayed with when he visited us in Palo Alto for one of those seminars. He stayed with that family and they were on pretty good terms, but the guy was scared to death of him. The idea of refusing to do what Erickson said — that didn't cross his mind. What power he had!

W: Well, as an explicit patient I saw Milton for only a couple of sessions, but I was scared. And to this day, I cannot tell you exactly what he did with me. I can only tell you that a great many things changed within a year and a half after I saw him. I came home and got out of my analytic treatment forever and decided that I would see what I could do on my own. That was the last time I had any therapy. Within a year, I had gone to the Far East to where my wife's people lived. And I had a major operation.

H: That's right. You had that heart operation that you hadn't decided about yet.

W: That's right. And our first child was conceived. That's a fair amount of things happening in a year. And I don't quite know how.

H: Did he discuss any of those things explicitly with you?

W: Well, it is going to sound a little strange, but I am not too clear about what we did discuss explicitly. I don't think that I was in a trance the whole time.

H: You are a good subject.

W: But something happened.

H: I am sure that there are things you remember.

W: Yeah. But I am not sure that even Milton could take care of the ravages of the next 20 years. I may have had more at one point and lost some of it.

Let's go back a minute to the fact that he could be rather stubborn about some things that were brought up. In a way, I think that is rather nice. Because the last thing that I think we would want to contribute to is the image of someone without flaw. Milton had his limitations and Milton was very human, thank God for that. He was not really the perfect guru sitting on the mountaintop by a long way.

H: Now, on his subject of hypnosis or influencing people, he was exceptional. But in other aspects of his life he was just an ordinary guy. He would only occasionally drop the professional attitude with us. Once or twice after a dinner, he was just a guy. But ordinarily he was in a professional stance with us, teaching us something all of the time. But he bragged a lot and he had his flaws, that's true.

W: He was just a man. Except for the bragging, he didn't pretend to be anything else.

H: No. The bragging was part of being just a man in the sense he would consider himself like others and then surmounted that.

W: There was one thing. I don't know if it is a flaw, but we did run into it a couple of times. If you will recall, a couple of times we approached him about his failures. Milton said, "Well, I would be glad to give you an example." And then he would give the example. But at the last moment, the failure would somehow turn into a success. Well, that may be a bit of a weakness but. . .

H: As he said at one point, he didn't see what you learned from talking about a failure unless you knew why it failed, and then you might learn something.

W: He did have, I think, a few highly fixed opinions, some of which I certainly saw differently. I remember him telling about cases where there was no point at all in trying to do something. I really don't see those cases that way now and I am not sure that I saw them that way then. But his opinion was rather heavy then or he just had some fixed ideas about those cases.

H: I think so. In fact, Don Jackson said something that I thought was rather wise. Erickson had mentioned a manic-depressive he didn't think was curable. And Jackson said, "Well, what he must mean is that with his technique he was not curable." And that had never occurred to me. That he couldn't reach him with his technique.

W: Well, people shouldn't put him up on a pedestal, cover him with white paint, and nail a halo up.

H: He would have been the first to object to that, I think.

W: That's correct. I am sure you will remember the demonstration he put on with the hot sauce. Even when we were just in a social situation, and he was just being a guy, he was still showing us that he was an extraordinary guy. We were in a Mexican restaurant and he said, "This isn't very hot. Bring me out something hotter." He did this two or three times, until the chef thought, "This will set him on fire." And he just had a spoonful of it, and licked it down, I presume with an anesthetized mouth done by self-hypnosis.

H: It had to be. Nobody could take that hot sauce with an ordinary tongue. But I think he did self-hypnosis ordinarily as part of his pain control, and then he did it as part of that hot sauce demonstration.

He always said that if he had any time at all, he could control the pain. When it took him by surprise, when the muscles wrenched away from the ligaments by surprise from cramps, he couldn't. But if he had a few minutes, he could do it. He had a lot of strength. I mean, he would take two or three hours to put himself together in the morning so that he could be comfortable. But once he got himself organized, then he would wear us out, hour after hour, talking. When we were ready to go, he was still going strong.

I was listening to a tape of Erickson with a guy (we'll call Dr. G) who was an Erickson disciple. Dr. G went down there to set up practice in Phoenix. He was setting up a beautiful office in a high rise down there, and he wanted to do it properly. He was talking to Milton about this. And Milton said, "Well, when I set up practice, all I had was this little room. I came down here to work in the state hospital and we had a falling out, so I left and I set up a practice sooner than I expected. I didn't have any furniture. All I had in this room was two chairs and a card table." So Dr. G said, "Well, that wasn't very much to set up practice." And Milton said, "Well, I was there." What more was necessary? And he absolutely felt that way. That is why he could work in a train station or an air terminal.

W: I remember stories about his going to Chicago and there was somebody that wanted to see him, so he had him come out to O'Hare Airport. He had half an hour and he talked to him right there in the airport lounge.

H: He used to do that. The only time that I saw him express any reluctance at the burden of being a therapist was once when he came to San Francisco. He worked at the workshop all day and at lunchtime he had to see a patient or two, and then at the end of the day there was a woman waiting to see him. He said something like, "My God. That's a lot." And then went off to see her. It was the only time I heard him object. Ordinarily, he would work all day, see people at lunch, see people before dinner, have dinner with his group, and then see a patient afterwards. And that was on his workshop days. Everywhere he went there were patients and they would take advantage of his visit to talk with him.

The case he was to see last, that day, was interesting to me because I knew the woman. I was trying to get patients of his and talk to them privately about what the therapy was. One of her problems was that she picked at her face and made sores. Also, she didn't like beans. So she had to put a can of beans in her bathroom by the mirror. She always picked her face in front of the mirror and if she picked at her face she had to eat the can of beans.

W: Tying two things together.

H: Milton had a sense of humor. So that most of the talking, that "grim" business of therapy was funny really, what they did, what he did, and the whole bizarre situation.

W: Well, I think we were probably rather important to him. I don't think there were many people he could let on to how humorous he found things or that he would rather spend most of his life sitting there seeing patients, seeing things that he thought were very humorous. He had to keep the lid on it completely and with most of his colleagues. He could begin to let us see.

H: I think that he was really looking forward to our visits. We brought ideas from outside and we were a great audience for him when he was telling about his cases.

I was thinking of that musician with the fat lip who used to come in and yell at him. The guy was angry at his father. And Erickson actually had the guy come in and yell. He couldn't play the horn because his lip swelled for psychosomatic reasons. The guy would come in and yell at him session after session. That was the one where he arranged an appointment without ever telling the guy about the appointment.

He said to the guy, "Well, let's see, this is May, isn't it?" And the guy said, "What do you mean, May. My God, don't you even know what month it is?" And then Erickson would say, "It must be about the 15th." The guy would say, "What do you mean, the 15th? It is the 10th. I've got a psychiatrist who doesn't even know what day it is." And then Erickson would say, "Well, it must be about four o'clock." "Four o'clock, it's only two o'clock."

At the end of the sessions, Erickson would open his book and say, "I am writing an appointment in and I want you to be on time," and he would close the book. And the guy would show up on June 15th at four o'clock. As long as he said that while the guy was shouting and it was dropped in inappropriately to what the guy was saying, the guy couldn't forget. And he also couldn't refuse to come in, because he never was told to come in. He couldn't be late because he had never been told an exact time where he could be late.

W: I seem to remember that in that case and in some others we would try to bring up something about the parallel between expressing anger at him and anger at his father. And Milton would just brush that aside. It was very curious what he would listen to and what he would just disregard.

H: We were trying to find out how he dealt with couples and families. Sometimes he saw them together and often he saw them separately.

W: That's right. We were looking for a policy, a common line.

H: At one point, he would say that the sexual symptom is absolutely a couple's case. That is the way he would treat it, like a couple. Another one he would treat individually, like Ann who had tremendous inhibitions; she went to bed and couldn't have sexual relations because she had all that choking and gasping. When he got her over that, we asked him, "What about the husband? Isn't there going to be some adjustment for the husband?" He said, "He'll have no problem adjusting." We said, "What do you mean?" He said, "Well, he rather passively accepted the way the wife was. Now that she has changed, he will accept the way that she is."

The fact that there was a contract between them wasn't what he was thinking in that case. And we were trying to emphasize that, and he was just puzzled by it, really. Whereas with another case, he would assume it was a contract. And we never knew which way he was going to jump.

I think that he partly hesitated to make a simple statement or a theoretical statement because it was too simple. The case was a metaphor; it contained all the ideas that he wanted to communicate. Any reduction of that case, down to a few sentences of description theoretically, would do violence to its complexity.

W: But have less in it than the story.

H: One of the things that was missing in a discussion with him was that he never referred to a teacher. I don't think he ever referred to doing something because some authority said so, or said, "I did this because I learned it from so and so." He presented everything as if it originated with him.

Usually, you draw from a previous authority to support what you say. Erickson absolutely never did that. He would say, "Try it and see if it works." He didn't even use himself as an authority in that sense. He didn't say, "Do it this way. Come back and tell me how you did it." That was why he wasn't a guru in the usual sense.

W: And yet at the same time, he would insist that people do the proper background study as he himself did. Therefore, it came out something like, "Get yourself properly trained and learn all that stuff carefully, and then go your way."

H: The whole thing about him not being a cult leader was that he absolutely was for diversification — everybody working in their own way, in their own style. So he didn't want us to imitate. And he didn't imitate anybody before him.

Gregory Bateson was considered a deviant in his own profession of anthropology. I think it is interesting that Erickson, who was a deviant in psychiatry, was admired by Bateson, who was a deviant in his field. Erickson actually admired Bateson very much. Neither one was at all concerned about conforming to the proper way according to his profession. They really were explorers of what they felt was relevant in life.

W: They both thought very similarly in that respect.

H: You know there was a case that sort of describes him. When he worked in that hospital in Eloise or somewhere, they had this violent woman who came in. And she said, "I am going to yell for a while and then I am going to break a few bones." And she yelled, and then she would stop and say, "I'm going to yell for a while and then I am going to break some bones." And they had about six aides who were afraid to take her on. They called for Erickson and he came and she yelled, "You better not touch me, Doctor. I am going to yell and break a few bones." And he said, "I won't touch you. I want you to go on yelling." So she went on yelling. And then he took a syringe. . . .

W: I think there is another step before. He said, "OK, yelling seems to be your job. I am not going to touch you, but is it all right with you if I just do my job?" And she said, "If you don't touch me, you go ahead and do your job." He got permission.

H: He took a syringe and when she had her mouth open yelling, he squirted it in her mouth and she swallowed it. Then she stopped yelling and she said, "Was that sleeping medicine, Doctor?" And he said, "Yes it was, but I didn't touch you, did I?" And she said, "No. You didn't." And then she said, "Now there is a doctor that knows his business."

6

Why Not Long-Term Therapy?
(1990)

It is curious how few meetings and training programs there are on how to do long-term therapy. Most of the announcements one sees are for seminars and workshops on brief therapy. The implication is that everyone knows how to engage clients in therapy for months or years. Yet long-term therapists are made, not born. Therapists do not have innate skills in committing clients to long-term contracts. Without training, they must learn by trial and error to do interminable therapy when they get into practice.

Often it is thought that long-term therapy occurs because the therapist does not know how to cure a person faster. A more respectful view is that it is a special ability. After all, many people do brief therapy because they lack the skill to keep clients coming for a long time. Little is written about long-term therapy techniques.

One of the few therapists with the courage to discuss how to keep a client in therapy and block him or her from going to someone else was Milton H. Erickson. For example, he proposed that a technique for preventing a client going elsewhere was to listen to him and respond, "I know how difficult it is for you to talk about this. If you had to go over it again with someone else, that would be even more painful." Erickson reported that such simple comments prevent clients from going to other therapists. More complicated techniques developed by Erickson to keep clients in therapy still remain secret.

The length of therapy is one of the most important issues in the field, and insurance companies now set the limits. Clinicians have some voice in this matter and should consider the issues. The first issue involves the needs of the therapist, and the second the needs of the client.

THE ISSUE FOR THE THERAPIST

Because therapy is both a calling and a business, the topic of how to keep someone in therapy can be embarrassing. The implication can be that the therapist wants to make money by seeing the client longer. It is best if we face facts. A therapist *does* make more money from a client who stays in therapy for years compared with a client who stays in therapy only a short time. The fact that more money is made should not be a reason to avoid workshops or instruction in long-term techniques.

If we accept the financial problem as something we must live with, what are the merits of long-term therapy for the therapist? Even if some therapists would rather not think about the positive side of interminable therapy, it should be discussed. Like having romantic affairs, many people would rather do it than talk about it at a public meeting.

At one time short-term therapists were on the defensive. Long-term therapists thought of themselves as "deep" and were confident, even arrogant. They liked to imply that brief therapy was a shallow, superficial endeavor. Brief therapists had to quote scientific outcome results to prove their success, pointing out that research did not show any correlation between length of therapy and successful outcome. Long-term therapists easily rejected such data as irrelevant. They pointed out that outcome results do not cause changes in therapy approaches in the field, which change only on the basis of fashion. Short-term therapy was simply condemned as not fashionable and not elegant in practice or theory. Now, with changes in insurance and HMO contracts setting limits on therapy length, the situation is reversed; long-term therapists are becoming defensive and brief therapists are bragging. One day we might even see long-term therapists desperately trying to bring science into the issue.

Young therapists won't recall the Golden Age of long-term therapy and might appreciate an example of a personal encounter to illustrate how it was in those days. I was once dining in a restaurant in Paris and began talking with an American couple who were sitting at the next table. When they asked what I did, I said I directed a therapy institute. The couple knew a lot about therapy since they were from New York. They were pleased to find we had something in common. The husband said he had been in therapy for 12 years, considering psychoanalysis to be therapy, and his wife had been in therapy for 8 years. Both of them had several sessions a week. I asked if therapy had solved their problems. They looked surprised at the question. "Of course not," said the gentleman, as if thinking the matter over for the first time. "We wouldn't still be going if it had." I asked them if they would recommend therapy to someone else. They said, "Of course we would. Everyone should be in therapy." I could see they had a therapist who knew his business.

In the discussion, I mentioned that 12 years seemed a long time to be in therapy. Rather defensively, the man asked me how long we did therapy at our Institute. I said, "We average about six interviews. With student therapists the average is about nine interviews." The couple looked at me, shocked, as if regretting they had begun this conversation. I found myself saying apologetically, "Well, that's only an average, we see some people a long time." I even added, to fill the silence, "Sometimes people come once a month, and so six sessions can take as long as six months." The couple became rather condescending and polite. The gentleman said that I must see a different class of clients than he was familiar with. I said defensively that we treated every wretch who knocked on our door. He said that I certainly could not be doing therapy with advertising executives like him and his wife. They are required to be in therapy for a long time because they feel so guilty about their work that they have to pay a lot of money to an analyst for years as a kind of penance. I had to agree that our therapy did not meet that special need because we did not have that size advertising industry in our area. The couple lost interest in me and began to look for an Italian to talk to.

I found myself defensive about doing effective therapy even though the people were saying their long-term therapy had not produced results. I also realized that I did not know how the therapists of this couple had kept them coming so many years without any improvement. There are thousands of therapists with that skill in the large cities. If they teach it, they do not do so in public workshops where all of us can learn. Perhaps it is secretly taught during personal therapy. I understand a training analysis in New York now averages seven years. That is quite a bit longer than the few months that Freud recommended. Perhaps the analysands are more obtuse these days and so require a longer analysis, but it might also be that they are being taught more secrets about how to contain people in therapy.

Now that fashions, and funding for therapy, have changed, people are beginning to be defensive about doing long-term therapy. The pendulum is swinging. As we examine therapy today, there have been remarkable changes in the last two decades. No longer do a few therapists deal with a few clients in distress. Therapy has become a major industry. Just as photocopying machines are flooding the world with paper, the universities are pouring out therapists of every species. There are psychologists, psychiatrists, social workers, educational psychologists, industrial psychologists, hypnotherapists, rational therapists, drug counselors, hospital therapists, marital therapists, family therapists of a dozen schools, and so on. These therapists rush out into offices and agencies everywhere. Part of the reason for this deluge is the publicity given to therapy in the mass media. In TV dramas the characters are in therapy and discuss it as part of life. Talk show hosts discuss their therapy, setting examples for the audience. Women's magazines have columns on the subject. TV and radio psychologists advise everyone to rush off and get therapy. "If only your husband will go into counseling, all will be well" is the cry of the radio psychologist heard by millions.

With therapy such a way of life, is it proper for a therapist to talk about how briefly it can be done? Isn't that like General Motors bragging about how quickly they can build a Cadillac? Or surgeons bragging about how short a time it takes them to do bypass heart surgery? In the early days of therapy when people were less affluent and there was no insurance, it seemed appropriate to be brief. Now with what it costs to become a therapist, obviously it is only fair to get a return on the investment. Not only is an expensive undergraduate degree necessary, and an expensive graduate degree, but there is postgraduate training. There is also typically the personal therapy expense. It is hoped that a personal therapy will somehow make a therapist more successful. (It is also a way to provide clients for the training staff who might not otherwise have them. Four analysands and four guilty businessmen seen several days a week is all a long-term therapist needs to avoid having to get more referrals for several years.) Besides academic costs, therapists must go to private institutes to learn the therapy skills they were not taught in the university. Seminars and workshops are required to keep up with the continuing education requirements. A therapy practice these days represents a large financial investment, and we must accept that and count it in the fee.

The therapist is not the only person who is being supported by the therapy fee. Just as there are 40 or 50 backup persons to support every soldier who is actually in combat, so the therapist is at the tip of a pyramid of support personnel. There are administrators of training institutes, supervisors, protective service personnel and judges, hospital and prison staffs, public agency case workers, teachers of abnormal psychology, systems theorists, journal editors, publishers, professional organization staff, licensing authorities, constructivists, and so on. Obviously, a therapy case must provide enough money to support not only the therapist and his family, but all the auxiliary personnel employed in the field.

Can the same income be made with short-term therapy as with lengthy therapy? Some brief therapists argue that it can be done but only if the therapist is willing to seek financial salvation through suffering. The effort required to keep the hours of the brief therapist filled is considerable. I once had a brief therapy private practice, and to equal the income of the long-term therapist required from three to four times as many referrals. A constant supply of clients is necessary because they are constantly changing. I can recall envying the long-term therapists who could schedule their hours a year in advance with confidence that the rent would be paid. In short-term therapy one recesses as soon as there is an improvement, and so a client is shifted to appointments every two weeks or once a month. What happens to that hour next week that must be filled? Perhaps a new referral will come in time, but perhaps it will not. Another talk to a PTA meeting might be necessary. Each decision about whether to have an interview becomes a moral decision, not a routine matter.

The style of short-term therapy is also more exhausting. A day is long, rather than leisurely. As an example, in a first interview the therapist must make the effort to clarify what is wrong and think of something relevant to do, all in an hour. He or she typically formulates a problem and gives a directive. The second interview reveals the response to the directive, which is then modified. By the third interview a positive improvement is taking place and sessions can be spaced more widely apart. The search for new clients begins. What a contrast that is to a long-term approach, where it takes three sessions to complete a history and three more to finish the genogram before one begins to think about what to do to solve the problem. How much easier it is to lean back and say,

"Tell me more about that" or "Have you wondered why it upset you that I was late today?"

Long-term therapy can be leisurely because it lacks a goal, but brief therapy requires that something be done to achieve some end. One cannot create a method and try to fit everyone into it. The therapist must innovate a special directive for each person. The long-term therapist needs to learn only one method and apply it. The therapist does what he did with the last person. If the client does not fit the method, another one will. How much more demanding it is to come up with an innovation or a variation in each case. Some brief therapists try to use a method for all cases, such as always telling the clients to stay the same, but such simplicity only works with a few cases.

The long-term therapists have all the best theories to rationalize their techniques and the length of their therapy. Not only has there been a hundred years of talking and writing about psychodynamic theory, but new fashions in philosophy are always available. One can easily step from theorizing about the unconscious to turgid discussions of epistemology, aesthetics, constructivism, chaos, and so on. If the theory is heavy, the therapy can be light, particularly when the theories are about what is wrong with people rather than what to do about changing them. Brief therapists are usually stuck with talking about what to do, which does not lead to profound ideological discussions. There is also not much literature on brief therapy compared with the 70,000 books and articles written about psychodynamic theory.

As another issue, brief therapists tend not to have a theory of resistance. They believe one gets what one expects, and such a theory interferes with gaining cooperation from a client. Long-term therapy has a theory of resistance, which excuses therapy being done forever to overcome that resistance. They also have the potent theory that if the client wants to terminate, he is resisting change and has not really improved, obviously needing more therapy. Long-term ideology has the therapist be the one who decides when therapy is over, not the client, so the length of therapy is in safe hands. Therapy does not end until the therapist is satisfied that the client is as near perfect as can be achieved in one lifetime.

One must also not overlook the importance of the therapist's self-image when choosing the type of therapy to be done. The brief therapist tends to have an image of himself or herself as harried and under stress. The long-term therapist has a look of boredom at times, listening so much to so few people. Not even the marital contract requires that much togetherness. Yet the long-term therapist also has a positive image as a wise philosopher, one who could offer the best advice if he chose to, but clients must decide for themselves. In a comfortable chair in a well-decorated office, preferably with a fireplace, the therapist patiently listens like a good friend to the clients who come to him for many years. Sometimes confrontation is necessary, but if so it is gently done, so the person will continue in therapy. The long-term therapist is loved by his clients. Usually the short-term therapist is not. There is not enough time for a romance. This kindly, loving, philosophical image is particularly appealing as a target image for young people coming out of school. Graduates hope for a private practice, though more and more of them must settle for a salary in an agency or hospital where they must do brief therapy.

THE ISSUE FOR THE CLIENT

Besides the merits of long-term therapy for the therapist, there is the question whether the client benefits most from long- or short-term therapy. We must also consider not only the client but also his or her support personnel in the family network. A scientific case report might clarify the matter.

I recall a woman who became upset when she married. She went into therapy as a result. Eighteen years later she was still in therapy. At that point, she divorced her husband. She also divorced her therapist. The last time I saw her she was considering marriage to another man. She was also thinking of going back into therapy. Can we say that the two decades of therapy had a positive or a negative effect? Would short-term therapy have been preferable in her case? Only intensive research can resolve this question. However, a few ideas are evident. On one side, the woman never had a marriage that was a dyad. She was in a triangle with her husband and her therapist all during her marriage, as many men and women in individual therapy are today. What did the therapy cost her husband? Not only is the expense of therapy over the years a steady drain on a household budget, but what of the personal cost? This husband had a wife whose experiences and ideas, even her intimate thoughts, were more likely to be communicated to another man rather than to him. If communicated to him, it was often after she had spoken to her therapist about it and so it was a twice-told tale with second-hand emotion. Each major event in her life, including childbirth and crises with the children, was shared with her therapist. The husband was labeled as secondary as an advisor to his wife and a parent to the children, while the therapist was the authority and expert on human relations whom she consulted.

For a different perspective on this triangle, we can consider the fact that the husband lived 18 years with a wife while paying another man to listen to her complain. This relieved the husband of that task, which some husbands might consider a positive result and others might not. There was also the agreement, confirmed with each therapy visit, that the wife was defective and the husband was not, since he did not go to a therapist. Therefore, their relationship was defined by an expert as one where the husband was superior and took care of a wife who was not quite adequate. The long-term therapist was, of course, thinking of the wife as fragile and needing his support or he would not have continued with the therapy for so many years. By the act of seeing the wife in therapy, he communicated to the marital couple that the wife was not normal like other people.

How difficult it is to choose brief or long-term therapy in such a case. A positive aspect is that the therapist helped the marriage continue for those many years. An 18-year marriage is an accomplishment in this age of easy divorce. Many wives who get upset after marriage and have brief therapy rather than long-term might break up with their husbands. If the marriage was stabilized by therapy, should that not be considered a positive effect? One must also consider the fact that some wives and husbands do not seek therapy because they wish to change, but for consolation. Often they feel they must stay married for financial reasons, or for the children. They ask of the therapist only that a miserable marriage be made more tolerable by reframing aspects of it and offering suggestions. Perhaps it is wrong to help people stay in an unhappy marriage, but often they ask for that service. A brief intervention to make a change will not satisfy them.

THE STIGMA ISSUE

One important factor about long-term therapy is that the practitioners do not consider being in therapy a stigma. They consider therapy good for everyone and the fact of being in therapy does not mean one is defective, or inadequate, in the eyes of others. In this framework are the growth therapists, or those who seek to increase human potential. They do not find anything wrong with a client except the human condition, and all human beings can grow and improve. Yet the growth therapist might be aware that the client in therapy should not try to run for president. It is still the popular assumption that "therapy" means that a person is defective and unable to deal with life's problems like normal people, particularly if therapy goes on and on for years.

Long-term therapy is usually defended with the argument that the client is fragile and needs support in meeting life's problems. In contrast, the brief therapist tends to have the view that all the person needs to become normal like other people is a few sessions to straighten out some problems. The underlying premise of brief therapy is fundamentally different from the long-term therapy view of the human condition and how people cope with it. A brief therapist, for example, might turn down someone for therapy because the person does not need it. Long-term therapists consider therapy valuable for everyone, and no one should be rejected if he or she can afford it.

AUXILIARY PERSONNEL

Only recently has the social context of a client been emphasized by therapists. The effect of the family organization is now more taken for granted. For example, suppose a kindly family member dies and the family becomes unstable. If a family member enters therapy with a kindly therapist, the family is stabilized. A problem only occurs when termination is considered. At that point the family will have to reorganize to adapt to the loss that they had not adjusted to. As the family becomes unstable, it is the client who will appear agitated, and the therapist will conclude he still has problems and must continue longer in therapy. As the years pass, the therapy has the function of stabilizing the family. Sometimes the same goal is achieved by regularly hospitalizing a family member, usually an expendable adolescent. The auxiliary personnel of the therapist, the hospital staff, and the auxiliary personnel of the client, the family, all benefit from the therapeutic arrangement. The family benefits by stability, the therapist and his auxiliary personnel benefit from the fee. Can we say that is not a proper function of therapy? Short-term therapy does not offer that function. In fact, short-term therapy tends to destabilize a family as part of inducing change. Long-term therapists tend to stabilize the organization the way it is.

There is another aspect of stabilization that involves symmetry in human relations. Just as human beings and other animals are symmetrical, having one eye above each side of the nose, one ear on each side of the head, and so on, there seems to be the same pattern in human interaction. This is called the 4th law of human relations. With a married couple, for example, if one spouse becomes attached to someone outside the family, the other may seek an attachment. That is, if one spouse begins an affair, the other spouse often seeks one also. Or the spouse might become overinvolved with people at work, or goes into therapy and attaches to a therapist. Similarly, if a spouse enters therapy, the other one can become attached to someone else as a way of balancing the symmetry of the family.

Within the family, if a mother becomes attached to her son, the husband is likely to become attached elsewhere, perhaps to his mother or a therapist. Obviously, if families need to balance symmetrically in this way, there must be therapists available to be paid to help correct the symmetry of the family. If the involvement of the family member with someone else is long-term, the spouse must have a long-term therapist to provide the needed stability for the system.

THE NEEDS OF THE INDIVIDUAL

Besides stabilizing an organization, what of the needs of the individual? Does long-term therapy meet those needs better than short-term therapy? Let us consider a basic human need: the need to hypothesize. Social psychologists have proposed for many years, and brain researchers are now suggesting, that a basic need of a person is to make hypotheses about himself and other people. One cannot *not* hypothesize. Whatever someone does, we must make a hypothesis about why the person did that. As this comment illustrates, we must even make hypotheses about why we hypothesize. In all our waking hours, if not in our dreams, we explain.

Does short-term therapy help with this need? Obviously it does not because it is not assumed that conversation about a problem will change the problem. Action must be taken. I recall years ago concluding that insight comes *after* a therapeutic change. When I did a brief intervention and got someone over a symptom, he or she wanted to tell me insightfully about all the functions of the symptom in the past and present. Even if I was not interested, the insight was imposed on me. I now realize that the person was fulfilling the need to hypothesize. People have to have an explanation of why they got over a symptom and so must rethink why they had it. Unaware of the hypothesizing need, I was impatient with them since the problem was over and they should go about their business.

When we examine long-term therapy from this view, obviously its greatest contribution is in the hypothesizing area. Hour after hour, week after week, month after month, year after year, the client has a therapist willing to sit and hypothesize. "I wonder why you are puzzled over what you did?" "Let us examine where that idea came from" or "Isn't it interesting that you. . ." Every hypothesis about the past and present is explored. The two people enjoy hypothesizing together, and each has needs satisfied. The therapist finds support for a theory that has as its foundation the need to hypothesize and explain. The clients must hypothesize to try to explain why their lives are always such a mess.

THE INTERPRETATION VERSUS THE DIRECTIVE

Long-term therapy primarily focuses on the interpretation, which is the tool of hypothesis making. Short-term therapy focuses on the directive, which is the tool for producing a change. Long-term therapy tends to be educative. Rather than focus on resolving a problem, the task is to help the person understand. With that emphasis, outcome research is not appropriate. There is nothing for the person to get over. In contrast, brief therapy usually focuses on a problem that is to be changed by the interventions. Whether the change occurs or not can more easily be determined. To put the matter in another way, long-term therapy tends to create an elite who have specialized knowledge about themselves that the average person does not have. The client learns to monitor himself and hypothesize why he does what he does within an ideological framework that is only learned in therapy. The short-term client tends to get over a problem and get back to being like other people rather than being special.

Long-term therapy ideas are easier to learn because they are part of the intellectual climate of the time and available in both professional and popular literature. Giving brief interventions, such as arranging an ordeal or a paradox, is more difficult to learn, since the specialized techniques are largely confined to the practitioners of therapy and are unknown to intellectuals generally. Perhaps that is why few long-term therapy workshops are needed and many are necessary to learn brief-therapy techniques. They cannot be learned merely by living in an intellectual culture.

SPECIAL PROBLEMS REQUIRING LONG-TERM THERAPY

Rather than create an either/or situation for long-term or brief therapy, one might suggest that there are times for long-term therapy and other times for brief interventions. Let us consider some of the situations where long-term therapy seems appropriate.

Besides the need to stabilize a married couple or a family over time, there are special problems. One serious problem is that of sexual or physical abuse, where therapy is usually mandated by the court. A brief intervention might stop those illegal or immoral acts. However, how can one be sure the acts have really stopped The possibility of a relapse is not an academic matter but means a victim will be harmed. There is a need to monitor these clients over time to be sure the positive effect of therapy continues. If one follows the person in a serious way, it becomes long-term therapy and is compelled by the nature of the problems.

Another type of problem usually requiring long-term therapy is the chronic psychotic and his family. With a first episode of psychosis, therapy can be brief since it is focused on getting the person back to normal functioning as quickly as possible. A crisis therapy with the family is designed to get a young person diagnosed schizophrenic off medication and back to work or school. This can be accomplished relatively quickly. However, if a therapist is dealing with a case where the person has been hospitalized a half-dozen times, the need for long-term therapy is apparent. The client is chronic, the family is chronic in that it expects the person to be incurable, and the professionals dealing with the client are in a chronic expectation that medication will be needed forever and custody regularly. To change all the auxiliary personnel in such a situation is obviously not a short-term task.

Another special problem is the long-term therapy that is done reluctantly when a therapist wants to terminate a person and cannot. So the therapy goes on without enthusiasm and even with resentment. In the same way, the client can wish to terminate and receives such a reaction from the therapist that he or she is unable to do so. One analogy in such a case is the addiction framework. Just as a person can become addicted to a lover, this can happen in therapy. The person might be hooked on a particular therapist or just on being in therapy with someone. A therapeutic goal is to successfully get the person free.

Perhaps it is in the nature of therapy that addiction occurs because of the kinds of sequences involved. In a typical addiction pattern there is a promise of feeling good and of intimacy, and this is followed by a rejection, which takes the form of not fulfilling the intimate promise. Yet it might still happen. It is like a mother encouraging her child to seek her out and then not responding because she is too busy. She invites the child and complains if he hangs on her. By the nature of the therapy contract, the situation is a relationship of an intimate nature. Yet the relationship cannot be consummated as an intimate relationship, and rejection is inevitable. The intimate rapport also lasts only as long as the person pays the bill; thus it is a paid friendship and so a rejection of intimacy while implicitly promising that. Often long-term therapists are caught up in such addictive relationships and cannot escape until a third party, such as a supervisor, helps detach them.

There are, of course, situations where long-term therapy is not appropriate and the therapist must work briefly. Therapy that is limited by an insurance company to a certain number of interviews is obviously not long-term, unless client or therapist decides to make a financial sacrifice and to continue the therapy. Another limited situation is the short-term hospitalization paid by insurance companies. The person is hospitalized for a few weeks and discharge will occur when the insurance runs out, no matter what. Usually the therapist who briefly sees the client inside the hospital cannot carry him or her outside and so continue the therapy.

FUTURE FINANCIAL ARRANGEMENTS

As we look over the field today and consider the long and the short of therapy, there are trends for which we must prepare. Obviously, therapy is going to become shorter because of the ways it is financed. Just as it was discovered that hospitalization could be more brief when the insurance companies decided that, so therapy will become briefer as insurance companies limit the length of therapy. Certain changes are going to come in the basic financing of the therapy enterprise and so new opportunities arise.

When we look at the history of therapy, the most important decision ever made was to charge for therapy by the hour. Historians will someday reveal who thought of this idea. The ideology and practice of therapy was largely determined when therapists chose to sit with a client and be paid for durations of time rather than by results.

When one realizes that charging by the hour was an arbitrary decision, there is no reason why other ways of financing therapy could not be developed. Long-term therapists might continue to use the hourly charge for clients who can personally finance that, but other therapists can consider alternate ways of charging.

CHARGING BY THE RELIEF OF THE SYMPTOM

Of the many ways to set a fee, the most obvious is to charge for the cure of a symptom rather than the number of hours sitting in the presence of the client. Each problem can have a designated fee. There is a precedent for this in medicine, where a surgeon charges by an action, in contrast to a pediatrician, who charges by the hour or any portion thereof as an office visit.

In the field of therapy there are also precedents. Masters and Johnson charge a flat fee for sexual problems, with consultation for a period of time afterward. Milton Erickson was known to say to parents who brought in a problem child, "I'll send you a bill when he is over the problem."

There are also people charging a fee per phobia rather than charging by the hour. I understand a group is charging $300.00 to cure any phobia. Anticipating quick results, they will continue to see a person for that fee until the phobia is gone. Another way we are already charging by this method is when we accept time-limited therapy by insurance companies. To see a client for only 20 interviews at a set fee is to charge a set price for the relief of a symptom. The difference is that if the therapist resolves the symptom in only three sessions, he or she cannot collect for the remaining 17 hours, as might be done with a flat fee.

What are the problems in setting a fee for the successful relief of a symptom? First, the therapist has to be able to resolve the problem. That is what everyone attending brief therapy workshops is learning to do. If brief therapy can be successfully taught, as the teachers claim, there is no reason that payment cannot be made on the basis of success. There will also be the need to protect both client and therapist with any price arrangement. The client might be offered a choice: payment by the hour into an uncertain future, or a flat fee for getting over a specific problem. The contract would have to be precise in problem and goal. What if there is an ambiguous outcome? One way to protect therapist and client would be to have an escrow account. The fee could be put into it until the problem is over. On those occasions when client and therapist disagree, an arbitrator can be available.

Such procedures can be worked out since they are simply part of setting up a new system. A more important issue is setting the fee. How much for relieving a depression, if that category is used? How much for solving school avoidance? What is the price to stop an alcoholic from drinking? If a person has several problems, can priorities be listed? There might also be contingency fees for relapses. These are important issues, and resolving them will bring more precision into the therapy field. There will need to be a manual rather different from the current DSM-III, which is irrelevant to therapy. Such a manual would essentially be a price-per-problem listing. One can hope that this arrangement will not lead to price cutting to compete for the insurance dollar. Obviously, the arrangement of payment per symptom will be met with enthusiasm by therapy contractors.

As this pricing system develops, most therapists will first think of correlating outcome with the number of hours to achieve the goal. In time it will be recognized that the issue is types of intervention rather than time. An example is the medication interview of a psychiatrist. Once they charged by the hour, sometimes regretting that they could not see more patients per hour, like other doctors. Then they discovered they could charge the same hourly fee for a medication interview and yet see clients for only 10 minutes. This increased their fee to six times the previous income per hour. Then the medication interview was set for a fee independent of hours. I know of one practitioner who has 60 medication interviews per day, charging what would once have been the fee for 60 hours. This can be a model for brief therapists. They might not achieve that large a number of clients per hour, but they can see clients for 10 or 15 minutes rather than an hour and so increase their income by several times.

Obviously there are a variety of ways of charging fees. The problem is complex, but it is solvable. A positive thought is that spontaneous remission is not uncommon and can be as high as 40% to 50%, according to waiting list studies. If that is so, therapists can be rather incompetent and still get a fee in almost half their cases, as they do now.

Once a few therapists have the confidence to charge on the basis of outcome, others will have to follow to stay in business. One important effect will occur in training programs as therapy requires more skill and becomes more brief and precise. It might ultimately be that teachers will be paid by particular therapy techniques successfully taught instead of being paid by the hour or the semester. Just as client fees can be determined by results, so can the fees for training.

At the moment it is the client who risks money and time by going to a therapist with no guarantee of change, no limit on the length of time of therapy, and no way of knowing the ultimate cost. When a fee is charged for the successful resolution of a problem, it will be the therapist who takes that risk. The therapist must either change someone or continue to see him or her for unpaid interviews while more lucrative clients are waiting. With the past arrangement of pay by the hour, it was the client who could go broke or waste hours, months, or years of his or her time in therapy. With the fee-for-a-problem arrangement, it is the therapist who can go broke or waste time. Is that not something we are willing to risk rather than impose it on clients, since we therapists are kindly and helpful people?

7

Zen and the
Art of Therapy
(1992)

Zen Buddhism is apparently the oldest continuing procedure in which one person sets out to change another. For at least 700 years, Zen masters have responded in a one-to-one relationship with someone who wishes to change. I will attempt to clarify the nature and influence of Zen on the ways of changing people in Western therapy, particularly in relation to the strategic, or directive, approach best represented by Milton Erickson.

For those pursuing the spiritual aspects of therapy, I should emphasize that here the focus is not on the spiritual side of Zen, but on the practical side of the art of changing people. That is, there is an interpersonal setting for spiritual development, which does not "just happen," just as therapeutic change does not "just happen." To achieve satori in Zen, one is not struck by enlightenment while sitting under the bo tree. A special relationship with a master is required, and a set of procedures, some of them bizarre, make up the interpersonal setting for spiritual growth. What I am emphasizing here is the materialist situation that frees an individual to develop spiritually. The actions to achieve enlightenment in Zen can be seen as similar to the actions that lead to change in strategic therapy.

The ideas of Zen influenced me in the 1950s when I was developing a therapy approach and doing research on the nature of therapy. For ten years, I was a member of Gregory Bateson's research project on communication where we investigated the paradoxes that occur because of the nature of classification systems. In 1953, the year I joined the project, I attended, with my colleague John Weakland, a series of lectures by

Alan Watts on "Eastern Philosophy and Western Psychology." Watts was the Director of the American Academy of Asian Studies at that time. An authority on Zen, he became an informal consultant on our project, since we shared the enthusiasm for paradox. Watts became interested in therapy as it related to Zen and later published a book on this topic (Watts, 1961). At that time, little was known about Zen, even in California where many philosophies flourished. Watts described himself as "back-door Zen," since he had not officially trained with a Zen master in Japan. His interests were both personal and intellectual, and his fascination with Zen was contagious.

In 1953, the same year we discovered Zen, I took a seminar on hypnosis from Milton Erickson and began to study his therapy. I found the premises of Zen to be just about the only way of explaining Erickson's directive therapy, which at that time was quite deviant in the field. As an apprentice of Erickson, I used ideas from Zen to understand his supervision.

I should make it clear that I am not an authority on Zen and that what I have to say about it is largely confined to its relevance to the field of therapy. There are also many different views, and schools, of Zen, ranging from ritualistic rites and bureaucratic procedures to sheer spontaneity. I am offering a view largely based on the ideas of Watts, which were in some ways deviant (just as Erickson was a deviant in the field of therapy and Gregory Bateson a deviant in the field of anthropology). For example, some authorities on Zen consider extensive meditation to be essential to enlightenment. Therefore, the path to satori can become a life of painful sitting while proctors hit the trainees with sticks if they go to sleep or into trance. Watts considered meditation personally important, but he saw these ritualistic procedures as ordeals imposed on trainees to help them discover that enlightenment occurs in other ways.

PERSPECTIVES ON ZEN

Zen Buddhism had its origins in India and traveled through China before being introduced into Japan in about 1200, when Zen monasteries were established there. A body of literature has grown up on this topic, even though it is the premise of Zen that one cannot achieve enlightenment by reading about it, but only by experiencing it personally. In Zen stories, there is an antiliterature, if not an anti-intellectual view. As an example, a woman who was a student of Zen died and left her son a letter in which she said: "There are 80,000 books on Buddhism and if you should read all of them and still not see your own nature you will not understand even this letter. This is my will and testament." Signed, "Your Mother, Not born, Not dead" (Reps, undated, p. 49).

A more typical example is the following Zen story (Reps, undated, p. 59).

The Zen master Mu-nan had only one successor. His name was Shoju. After Shoju had completed his study of Zen, Mu-nan called him into his room. "I am getting old," he said, "and as far as I know, Shoju, you are the only one who will carry on this teaching. Here is a book. It has been passed down from master to master for seven generations. I also have added many points according to my understanding. The book is very valuable, and I am giving it to you to represent your successorship."

"If the book is such an important thing, you had better keep it," Shoju replied. "I received your Zen without writing and am satisfied with it as it is."

"I know that," said Mu-nan. "Even so, this work has been carried from master to master for seven generations, so you may keep it as a symbol of having received the teaching. Here."

The two happened to be talking before a brazier. The instant Shoju felt the book in his hands, he thrust it into the flaming coals. He had no lust for possessions. Mu-nan, who never had been angry before, yelled: "What are you doing?"

Shoju shouted back: "What are you saying?"

This antiliterature view contrasts sharply with the intellectual tradition of Western therapy where something is said to be true only if a reference can be made to a previous authority, or prophet, who had written it. Yet it is reminiscent of the teachings of Milton Erickson. He rarely quoted past authorities and never as evidence that something was true. He did not say that something was so because a previous authority had said it was so. In a pragmatic American way, he said, "It is so, and if you try it, you will find that out." Although this kind of pragmatism was often misunderstood by clinicians who came from the European tradition of scholarship, it is typical of Zen.

The goal of Zen is satori, or enlightenment, which is assumed to come about in relation to a teacher who, when successful, frees the student from a preoccupation with the past or the future (or with trying to become enlightened). The relevance of Zen to therapy becomes apparent when one observes that Western ideas of psychopathology are extreme versions of the problems of the average person dealt with in Zen. The client in distress is typically said to be preoccupied with the past, with guilts, obsessions, or desires for revenge. Or the client can be overpreoccupied with the future, as with anxieties and phobias about what might happen. He or she struggles to control his or her thinking, wanting to be rid of certain thoughts. Sometimes the client fears death and sometimes the client seeks it, being so depressed about living. Interpersonally, the client is often so attached to a person, either in anger or love, that it is like an addiction. Sometimes the person is fixed on material possessions or compulsively works and never enjoys a nice day. By definition, a symptomatic person keeps repeating behavior that causes distress while protesting that he or she would rather not be doing so and cannot help it. These kinds of foci and fixations are assumed in Zen to be preventing a person from fully experiencing the present moment, which is one way to view enlightenment.

ZEN AND ERICKSON'S THERAPY

In the 1950s when Zen ideas began to enter the clinical field, there could not be a comparison with therapy. The psychodynamic ideology, which was what was available, contained premises so opposite from Zen that the two approaches could not be related. The focus on insight was in sharp contrast to the Zen focus on action. However, one therapist was establishing a therapy with a different set of ideas. Milton Erickson was known as the leading medical hypnotist of that time, and he was practicing a therapeutic approach that was new and was based on an ideology different from that of psychodynamic theory.

When I began to practice therapy in the mid-1950s and sought supervision from him, Erickson was the only therapist I knew about who had a new set of premises relevant to brief therapy. I also realized that one way to understand his directive therapy, which was incomprehensible in the nondirective psychodynamic framework, was to view it within the framework of some of the ideas of Zen. I talked to Erickson about the similarities between his work and the approach of Zen. His response was typical: He gave me case examples. These stories illustrated some of his views on the attempt to live in the present moment. For example, he described a case in which he hypnotized a golfer. The golfer was instructed to live only in the present moment and so focus total attention on one shot at a time. When the man next played golf, he was aware only of each shot. On the 16th hole, he was shooting his best game, but he did not know what his score was or what hole he was on. He was aware of only the present moment and not of the context.

PSYCHOPATHOLOGY IN TERMS OF
CLASSIFICATION SYSTEMS

A basic characteristic of human beings is that we are classifying animals. In fact, it appears that we cannot not classify. We must hypothesize about and categorize whatever is, or is not, happening. Past social psychology experiments and current brain research (Gazzanaga, 1985) suggest that we constantly make hypotheses; perhaps there is a nodule of the brain devoted to that. Since we must classify, we are vulnerable to the nature of classification systems. There are several important factors about classification related to the therapy field.

When we create a class, we automatically create other classes. If we create the classification "good," we also produce the class of "bad," as well as those of "not so bad" and "not so good." If something is "high," something must be "low." It is in the nature of classification that one cannot have the figure without the ground to contrast it — in fact, multiple grounds or other classes. Therefore, a person pursuing a class creates the opposite class, even when not wishing to do so, as when pursuing happiness, one creates unhappiness. Lao-tse put it this way, "When everyone recognizes goodness to be good, there is already evil. Thus to be and not to be arise mutually."

Another consequence of a classification system is that paradoxes inevitably are generated. This happens when the class of items conflicts with the item in the class. If a person says, "Disobey me," the responder cannot classify that in a way that allows either obedience or disobedience. The person who disobeys is obeying as instructed. To obey requires disobeying. Paradoxes of this kind are generated by the nature of classification systems (Whitehead & Russell, 1910), and human beings must deal with them. The classification problem has been recognized since Epimenodes said, "If a man says he is lying, is he telling the truth?" Another aspect was emphasized by Korzybski and the general semanticists. Once something is classified, we tend to respond to all the items within the class as identical when they are not. The phobic responds to each phobic situation as identical to every other. As Korzybski liked to point out, "Cow 1 is not Cow 2" (Korzybski, 1941).

Changing a person means changing the person's classification system. Individuals have difficulty changing on their own because they think within that system. The task is given to therapists and to Zen masters to induce change. For example, a person who wishes to stop being constantly preoccupied with particular thoughts or actions tries not to think of them. It is the act of trying not to think of them that creates the class whose items one must think about in order not to think of them. It is like trying not to think of an elephant. A person wishing to be liberated and to behave more freely can try to achieve that by deliberately attempting to be spontaneous. Yet a person who tries to be spontaneous must fail, since spontaneous behavior is a class that does not include the item "trying." It is like trying to free-associate when the fact that one is directed to do so means it is not "free," but "purposeful." Similarly, if a person tries to be tranquil, it is like trying to try, since tranquility is a class of behavior that requires not trying. The more one tries to be tranquil, the less tranquil one becomes. As another aspect of the problem, if one tries to change oneself when the way one classifies is what must be changed, each attempt to change activates the classification framework, which prevents change. Like the self-corrective system of systems theory, the attempt to change is what activates the governors that respond to prevent change.

An inevitable problem in therapy and Zen is how to change a person when to do so means changing how the person classifies the helper who is trying to change that system. By asking for help, the client classifies the relationship between himself or herself and the therapist in a certain way, as being unequal. The goal of therapy is to achieve the point where the client is defined as equal to the therapist in that the client does not need help. The client is to become a peer, rather than a supplicant who asks for help. Yet how can the therapist change the helping relationship to one of equality when every act of help, guidance, giving interpretations, or giving a directive defines the relationship as unequal and the client as being helped by a helper? The acts of helping a person to change mean defining the relationship as not changed. The therapist, or Zen master, must influence the person to change "spontaneously" and so escape the helping relationship. This is the essential paradox of Zen and of therapy. One solution is the example of a student who attempted again and again to answer a Zen master's koan, only to be informed each time that he was wrong. Finally, he simply sat down beside the teacher. That was the answer, since he was behaving as an equal.

Many Zen anecdotes illustrate the problem of changing classification. Reps (undated, p. 11) provides a subtle example.

Just before Ninakawa passed away, the Zen master Ikkyu visited him. "Shall I lead you on?" Ikkyu asked.

Ninakawa replied, "I came here alone and I go alone. What help could you be to me?"

Ikkyu answered: "If you think you really come and go, that is your delusion. Let me show you the path on which there is no coming and no going."

With his words, Ikkyu had revealed the path so clearly that Ninakawa smiled and passed away.

SYSTEMS THEORY AND ZEN

In the 1950s, the cybernetic revolution was influencing the field of therapy by introducing the ideas of self-corrective systems. Erickson had been a participant in the first Macy Conference in the late 1940s and he was familiar with systems theory. The relevance of this to Zen appears with the basic premise of Zen that human beings are trapped on the wheel of life and keep repeating distressing behavior. The more a person attempts to escape from this destiny, the more he or she is caught up in it because the attempts to change cause the system to continue. One goal of Zen is to free the person from the repeating system so that new, spontaneous behavior can occur. Obviously, that is also the goal of therapy. It is the assumption of Zen that the attempt to change, or help, causes the reaction that prevents change or help. Obviously, that is the assumption of a cybernetic, self-corrective system. As any element moves toward changes in the parameters of the system, a reaction occurs that prevents the change. How to change without activating the forces that prevent change is the paradox of both Zen and therapy. It requires an almost trickster approach to free the person from preventing change. As an example, how can one obey a teacher who is instructing one to think independently and not to obey teachers?

As part of the trickster aspect of enlightenment, both Zen masters and Erickson have been accused of being too concerned with interpersonal power and manipulation. In both situations, the need of a teacher to have power and skill in influencing people is simply assumed. As an example, Erickson liked to describe how someone in an audience called out that he could not be hypnotized and he defied Erickson to try. Erickson shifted the issue to whether the person was able to refuse to do what he was told. When the person insisted he could refuse, Erickson told him to come up the right aisle and sit beside him on his left. In defiance, the person came up the left aisle and sat beside him on his right. Erickson continued to induce a trance, assuming that is what the man wanted (Haley, personal communication).

There is a Zen story one cannot read without thinking of Erickson (Reps, undated, p. 8).

The Master Bankei's talks were attended not only by Zen students, but by persons of all ranks and sects. . . . His large audiences angered a priest of the Nichiren sect because the adherents had left to hear about Zen. The self-centered Nichiren priest came to the temple, determined to debate with Bankei.

"Hey, Zen teacher," he called out. "Wait a minute. Whoever respects you will obey what you say, but a man like myself does not respect you. Can you make me obey you?"

"Come up beside me and I will show you," said Bankei.

Proudly, the priest pushed his way through the crowd to the teacher.

Bankei smiled. "Come over to my left side."

The priest obeyed.

"No," said Bankei, "we may talk better if you are on the right side. Step over here."

The priest proudly stepped over to the right.

"You see," observed Bankei, "you are obeying me and I think you are a very gentle person. Now sit down and listen."

One problem in helping a person who seeks help, or a person who seeks enlightenment, is that to help that person one must change his or her way of life of constantly seeking help. I recall Watts telling a story of a Zen master who wished to inform his students that he could not enlighten them by teaching them something new. All the knowledge they needed to become enlightened was within them, so he could only help the students discover what they already knew. He said to a student, "You already know anything I could teach you." The student assumed that this was a wise master withholding, for some educational reason, important truths. The student could not escape from the classification of himself as a student, yet that was the goal of the relationship.

ZEN, ERICKSON, AND SELF-MONITORING

In the 1950s, I began to find similarities among Zen, systems theory, and the therapy of Erickson. There was a way to describe human problems and an ideology for therapy that was an alternative to psychodynamic theory and practice. It was also different from the learning theory therapies that developed later. One dissatisfaction with psychodynamic therapy was the growing realization that people were being created who spent their lives monitoring themselves and hypothesizing why they did what they did. The constant preoccupation with exploring one's past and watching out for unconscious conflicts led to an extreme self-consciousness. In the attempt to use self-exploration and awareness as a way to avoid distress, people became preoccupied with their distress and its origins. Supposedly the self-preoccupation was to free people from the past, but such a change was not occurring. After years of therapy, people were habitually monitoring themselves. Even while having sexual relations, they would be wondering why they were enjoying the experience.

In contrast, Milton Erickson came from the tradition of the unconscious as a positive force. One should give up trying to monitor one's unconscious consciously and allow it to direct one's actions. The centipede should not attempt consciously to coordinate its 100 legs. Erickson's goal was to have people respond to their impulses in the present without being concerned about whether or how they were doing so. In the same way, the primary goal in Zen is simply to live rather than to be preoccupied with how one is living. The goal is to recover from self-monitoring. In fact, it is said, "When you are really doing something, you are not there." As an example (Reps, undated, p. 18):

> Tanzan and Ekido were once traveling together down a muddy road. A heavy rain was still falling. Coming around a bend, they met a lovely girl in a silk kimono and sash, unable to cross the intersection, "Come on, girl," said Tanzan at once. Lifting her in his arms, he carried her over the mud.
>
> Ekido did not speak again until that night when they reached a lodging temple. Then he no longer could restrain himself. "We monks don't go near females," he told Tanzan, "especially not young and lovely ones. It is dangerous. Why did you do that?"
>
> "I left the girl there," said Tanzan. "Are you still carrying her?"

The goal of therapy is to change someone's actions or to change the ways the person classifies actions and thoughts as bad or good, painful or pleasant, useful or not useful, and so on. Rational advice does not usually solve such a problem. The change must occur in action, according to Zen. One way is for the master to direct the person in some action and resolve the problem as part of that activity. As a result, Zen is often structured as a joint activity between master and student in some type of art. Often, it is taught through archery, swordsmanship, or the tea ceremony. There is a task, and the student associates with the master as part of the task. In that process, the master is directing what happens, rather than merely reflecting with the student.

As an example, one way to practice Zen is to apprentice to a master swordsman. A student who did that was given the task of cleaning the floors of the master's house. As he swept the floor, the student was surprised by the master's suddenly hitting him with a broom from around a corner. This happened again and again. No matter how the student anticipated where the blow of the broom would come from next, and got set to defend himself, he was hit with the master's broom. At a certain point, the student learned that he was best prepared to defend himself from some surprising direction by being unprepared in any direction.

Then he was ready to receive a sword. He had begun the move toward enlightenment in the context of action between teacher and student. Zen masters pride themselves on being responsive in any direction. Watts told me of one who asked another, "What do you know of Zen?" The other immediately threw his fan at the man's face, and the man tilted his head just enough for the fan to fly by, and he laughed. (Once when Watts was visiting my home, my wife asked him, "What is Zen?" Watts happened to be holding a box of matches and he threw it at her. I don't know if she became enlightened, but she became angry.)

This active involvement of master and student in a task contrasts sharply with traditional psychodynamic, nondirective therapy. When I searched for a therapy relevant to Zen, I found that the directive therapy of Erickson included activities he set up between himself and the client, just as Zen master and student related around an activity.

As an example, a mother brought her 50-year-old son to Erickson, saying that he would do nothing and that he constantly bothered her, not even leaving her alone to read a book. Erickson said that the son could use exercise, and he suggested that the mother drive the son out into the desert and push him out of the car. Then she was to drive one mile and sit and read her book in the air-conditioned car while the son walked in the hot sun to catch up with her. The son would have no alternative except to walk. The mother was pleased with this task, but the son was not. After some time walking his mile in the desert, the son asked Erickson if he could not do some other exercise while his mother read her book. When he suggested that he would rather go bowling, Erickson agreed. Erickson pointed out to me that his use of classification in this way was calculated; the son would reject walking in the desert, but when he protested and wanted something else, he would remain within the classification of exercise and choose another exercise (Haley, personal communication). This example is typical of Erickson's way of getting into a relationship of action with a problem client, as is done in Zen.

Traditional therapy was based on a theory of psychopathology. Symptoms, thoughts, and character were classified according to a diagnostic system that was shared by clinicians and differentiated them from other people. A little girl who would not eat was classified as a case of anorexia nervosa, not as a little girl who would not eat. The language of psychopathology set clinicians apart from those who thought of human problems as dilemmas that arise in life. In contrast, a directive therapist prefers to think of problems as temporary, as a fluctuation in normal living that must be corrected. For example, when I was testing families of different kinds, it was necessary to select a normal sample. I found that I could not use clinicians to select normal families because they never found one. They always discovered some psychopathology in a family. It was characteristic of Erickson that he emphasized problems of living rather than pathological states. Instead of describing a child as having a school phobia, he would emphasize the problem as one of avoiding school, and he would have a way of dealing with that. He did not call a woman an agoraphobic, but a person who could leave the house only under special circumstances.

One problem in finding similarities between Zen and therapy is that in Zen there is no psychopathology. There are simply problems on the road to enlightenment. It is particularly significant that in Zen there is a way of classifying and dismissing human dilemmas that clinicians might consider serious psychopathology. In Zen, hallucinations, fantasies, and illusory sensations are called "makyo." It is said (Kapleau, 1989, p. 41), "Makyo are the phenomena — visions, hallucinations, fantasies, revelations, illusory sensations — which one practicing zazen is apt to experience at a particular stage in his sitting. . . .These phenomena are not inherently bad. They become a serious obstacle to practice only if one is ignorant of their true nature and is ensnared by them." Describing the phenomena further, hallucinations are said to be common, whether verbal or auditory, as are other sensations. "One may experience the sensation of sinking or floating, or may alternately feel hazy and sharply alert. . . .Penetrating insights may suddenly come. . . .All these abnormal visions and sensations are merely the symptoms of an impairment arising from a maladjustment of the mind with the breath." The author adds,

> Other religions and sects place great store by the experiences which involve visions of God or deities or hearing heavenly voices, performing miracles, receiving divine messages, or becoming purified through various rites and drugs. . . . From the Zen point of view all are abnormal states devoid of true religious significance and therefore only makyo. . . .To have a beautiful vision of a Buddha does not mean that you are any nearer becoming one yourself, any more than a dream of being a millionaire means that you are any richer when you awake.

The phenomena that could lead to a diagnosis of psychopathology are assumed, in this view of Zen, to be a product of the special situation of the person and will change as that situation changes. That is also the view of a strategic approach to therapy: such phenomena are a response to a situation and not a character defect or a permanent malady.

CHANGE IN ZEN

A strategic approach to therapy has no single method that is applied to all problems. Each case is considered unique and requires a special intervention for that person. Similarly, in Zen there is no method that is used to enlighten everyone who comes. There are standardized procedures, such as meditation, but it is assumed that a unique intervention must be made for enlightenment to be achieved. In a similar way, in a strategic approach to therapy, there might be standardized interviewing, but the directive must fit the unique situation. In Zen, learning and cognition are not considered the path to enlightenment. One is not taught how to live or instructed how to relate to others. In addition, neither strategic therapy nor Zen is based on the theory of repression. Therefore, insight into unconscious dynamics is not considered necessary to change nor is the expressing of emotions a goal. It is assumed that expressing emotions, like expressing anger, leads to more expressions of emotions and so to more anger.

In Zen, change is described as sudden and discontinuous, not as cumulative and step-by-step, as when learning or being educated. Similarly, in strategic therapy, the client is not educated by being taught to behave in a certain way or taught how to be a spouse or a parent. Nor is the Zen student taught how to become enlightened, and, in fact, one discovers that one must give up theories about it to achieve it. The assumption is that when the situation is changed by an intervention, the behavior will be appropriate to that new organization without ritual learning.

One of the characteristics of Erickson's therapy was the use of imagery. Often he would have a client image a scene in the past or in the present and use it to induce change. Such imaging might seem unrelated to Zen practice, where the focus is on reality, but a Zen story describes a wrestler named Great Waves who was of champion caliber in private training, but was so bashful that he lost all public bouts. He went to a Zen master for help (Reps, undated, p. 11).

"Great Waves is your name," the teacher advised, "so stay in this temple tonight. Imagine that you are those billows. You are no longer a wrestler who is afraid. You are those huge waves sweeping everything before them, swallowing all in their path. Do this and you will be the greatest wrestler in the land." The young man did that to the point where, "Before dawn the temple was nothing but the ebb and flow of an immense sea." The next morning, the master said to him, "You are those waves. You will sweep everything before you." And he did.

There is another similarity to Erickson's therapy that could be emphasized. In Zen, there are stories, or analogies, told over the centuries to illustrate the path to enlightenment. Erickson also told stories to illustrate his view of changing people. In both cases, education is accomplished with analogies and metaphors. As an example, Erickson liked to tell of an experience he had when he was 17 years old. He was totally paralyzed by polio and his doctor said he would not live until morning. Erickson asked his mother to arrange a mirror so that he could see the sky outside the window. He wished to enjoy his last sunset.

How similar that is to a parable Buddha told in a sutra (Reps, undated, p. 22).

A man traveling across a field encountered a tiger. He fled, the tiger after him. Coming to a precipice, he caught hold of the root of a wild vine and swung himself down over the edge. The tiger sniffed at him from above. Trembling, the man looked down to where, far below, another tiger was waiting to eat him. Only the vine sustained him.

Two mice, one white and one black, little by little started to gnaw away the vine. The man saw a luscious strawberry near him. Grasping the vine with one hand, he plucked the strawberry with the other. How sweet it tasted!

When we compare Zen with other therapies, we can think of examples where it is difficult to find parallels. We can turn to the Zen metaphor of Gutei's finger (Reps, undated, p. 92).

Gutei raised his finger whenever he was asked a question about Zen. A boy attendant began to imitate him in this way. When anyone asked the boy what his master had preached about, the boy would raise his finger.

Gutei heard about the boy's mischief. He seized him and cut off his finger. The boy cried and ran away. Gutei called and stopped him. When the boy turned his head to Gutei, Gutei raised up his own finger. In that instant the boy was enlightened.

When one examines different schools of therapy to find a case similar to this painful removal of a finger, it is difficult to do so, particularly in this age of litigation. If one existed, it would be a case of Erickson. One of his classic cases comes to mind (Haley, 1986, p. 197).

A mother came to Erickson saying that her adolescent daughter had stopped going out of the house. She would not go to school or see her friends because she had decided that her feet were too big. The girl would not visit the office and so Erickson visited the home on the pretext that the mother was unwell and that he needed to examine her as a physician. When he arrived at the house, he observed that the girl's feet were of normal size. He examined the mother, asking the girl to help him by holding a towel, and he maneuvered the girl so that she was standing beside him. Suddenly, he stepped back and trod on her foot as hard as he could. She yelped in pain. Erickson turned angrily to her and said, "If you would grow those things big enough for a man to see, I wouldn't be in this difficulty." That afternoon, the girl told her mother that she was going out and she went to visit friends and returned to school. Apparently, she was enlightened.

In this case and the Zen example, it is assumed that a sudden intervention causes change, that inducing pain can be a necessary part of an intervention in some cases, and that no education or cognitive and rational discussion is needed.

Related to this example is the use of ordeals, which are commonly part of both Zen and Erickson's work. The path to enlightenment is often painful, with an ordeal sometimes arranged by the master and sometimes voluntarily by the student, such as suffering hunger and cold.

With all the similarities between a strategic approach to therapy and Zen, one might wonder if there are differences. There are many, of course. For one, there is often a long-term involvement of years in Zen. Strategic therapy is briefer. Also, a primary difference is the remuneration to the therapist. One does not find therapists in yellow robes with begging bowls. They have reconciled financial success and therapy as a calling. There is also no emphasis on meditation in therapy; the activity is conversation and directives. One other difference is that strategic therapy has its origins in hypnosis, and practitioners often use trance to achieve their ends. In Zen, if one is meditating and goes into a trance, one is hit with a stick, since trance is not a goal of the interaction with a teacher. However, one might note that Erickson did not encourage meditating trances, but active responses.

There is also no family approach in Zen. Monks typically live with each other, not in families. Interventions by masters do not change families to change the individual. Once enlightened, the Zen monk might marry and live in a family, but the task of Zen is not to change a family constellation.

One important similarity is the use of humor in Zen and in therapy. There are many Zen stories that are amusing, and a characteristic of Erickson's therapy was his humor and practical jokes. Related to humor is the Zen use of koans and Erickson's use of riddles. Both techniques seem designed to help a trainee change perspective and to recover from being rigid and intellectual. When dealing with a client who believed that change was not possible, Erickson would pose a riddle that seemed impossible to solve. Then he would show the obvious solution. One riddle he liked was that of diagramming how to plant ten trees in five straight rows, four trees in each row, without lifting the pen off the paper. When the client tried and failed to do it, Erickson would show how simple the answer was if one can escape from rigid and stereotyped ways of classifying.

In the same way, and apparently for the same purpose, Zen masters build much of their work around koans and such impossible riddles. "What is the sound of one hand clapping?" is an example. One that provokes action rather than tranquil reflection is the koan where the master holds a stick over the trainee's head and says, "If you say this stick is real, I will hit you. If you say it is not real, I will hit you. If you don't say anything, I will hit you." The student must solve that koan or be hit. Such examples make one wonder whether much of Zen might not have been created to cure young Japanese intellectuals of being so self-conscious and rational.

Perhaps the most basic similarity between strategic therapy and

Zen is the willingness to make use of the absurd to change logical classification systems. Not only are absurd riddles and koans used, but absurd actions are demanded. With particularly rational and logical clients, Erickson would give them absurd tasks (Haley, personal communication). He would tell an overrational, intellectual person, for example, to go exactly 7.3 miles out into the desert, and there to park the car carefully, get out of it, and find a reason for being there. I have replicated this technique with overly logical scientists by sending them a certain distance up a mountain road to find a reason for being there. When they come back, they are different. Erickson's directive to climb Squaw Peak might have had similar purposes. It should be noted that when Erickson sent clients into the desert, they always went, and always found a reason for being there. When they came back, they were different—less rational and less logical, and perhaps more spiritual.

SUMMARY

In summary, what are the procedures of Zen that are relevant to therapy? In Zen, enlightenment is sought through a relationship with a master who believes that change can be sudden and discontinuous; who becomes personally involved with the student; who joins the student in a task that involves directing him or her; who attempts to escape from intellectualizing about life or monitoring personal behavior; who poses impossible riddles and insists on solutions; who approaches each student as a unique situation; who has a wide range of behavior and many techniques, including a willingness to be absurd; who focuses on the present and not the past; who solves the systemic problem that attempting to change prevents change; and who, within a kindly framework, uses ordeals to force a change. These are also the characteristics of a strategic approach to therapy.

If we take a broad view of the task of changing people, Zen practitioners and therapists have much to offer each other. Clearly, Zen came first, by a few hundred years. However, even though a latecomer, therapy has developed many innovations in recent years. When we take a broader view of enlightenment, we see that Erickson was not simply a unique therapist. He was working in a centuries-old tradition of masters sending people out into the desert to discover new ways of spiritual being.

REFERENCES

Gazzanaga, M. S. (1985). *The social brain,* New York: Basic Books.
Haley, J. (1986). *Uncommon therapy,* New York: Norton.
Kapleau, P. (1989). *The three pillars of Zen,* New York: Doubleday.
Korzybski, A. (1941). *Science and sanity* (2nd ed.), New York: The Science Press.
Reps, P. S. (undated). *Zen flesh, Zen bones,* New York: Doubleday.
Watts, A. (1961). *Psychotherapy East and West,* New York: Random House.
Whitehead, A. N., and Russell, B. (1910–1913). *Principia mathematica, (3 vols.),* Cambridge, England: Cambridge University Press.

8

Erickson Hypnotic
Demonstration: 1964
(1993)

This is a presentation of the text of an hypnotic demonstration by Milton H. Erickson, M.D., in 1964. At a medical meeting he hypnotized a series of volunteer subjects, and it is one of the few demonstrations of this type which was filmed. In 1972 Erickson was shown the film and asked to comment on why he did what he did in the hypnotic inductions. This paper presents the full transcript of the demonstration, along with Erickson's comments upon it, and my own discussion of it. The emphasis is upon hypnosis from the communication point of view.

Over the years, Milton H. Erickson, M.D., conducted many hypnotic demonstrations at seminars and medical meetings. Occasional audiotapes were made of these demonstrations, but he was rarely filmed in those early years when he was in his prime. There was no videotape available at that time, and 16 mm film was expensive. Without film, there was no opportunity to carefully analyze the visual as well as the audio presentation of his hypnotic work.

In 1964, at a meeting of the American Society for Clinical Hypnosis in Philadelphia, Erickson did an hypnotic demonstration for a medical audience. It was apparently kinescoped, the process prior to videotape, and later that was turned into an edited 16 mm film, which was technically poor in sound and picture, with parts cut out. Erickson gave me the copy of the film, and for a number of years I used it to teach his approach to hypnosis. Because of many questions I had about what he did in that demonstration, I took the film to Phoenix in 1972 and showed it to him, asking him to explain why he did what he did during the demonstration.

My own interest has been in understanding the hypnotic process in terms of communication, and this film provides the opportunity to both see and hear what Dr. Erickson said and how the subject responded. For example, when he tells a subject to awaken and the subject is puzzled as to why her hand stays up in the air, I am puzzled as well. It requires careful study of the film to develop an hypothesis about just what Erickson said when he appeared to awaken her but did not awaken her. Obviously, the hypnotic communication interchange is a complex and intricate one that is worth examining again and again when it is on film.

In this presentation, I will offer the text of the film and my later conversation with Erickson about it. I will also add my own comments about what I believe he was saying and doing. It might seem presumptuous of me to offer my own explanation, particularly when it differs from that of Erickson, but I think it is justified. At the time of this discussion, it had been 20 years since I attended my first seminar with Erickson, and I had spent hundreds of hours talking with him about hypnosis and therapy as part of my research. Therefore, I was familiar with many of his ideas. I have also done many research interviews with therapists, and I often found that what they considered themselves to be doing could be seen in a quite different perspective by an outsider who is examining the interview.

Another reason for adding my own comments is that Erickson's memory of this demonstration was limited because he had been ill at the time. As the discussion progressed, he seemed to remember more about it. The reader here can keep the opinions separate since I present them in different typestyles. In my comments, I might point out some things that seem elementary to an experienced hypnotist, but I think it helps most readers to understand what is happening. In his comments on this film, Erickson is not talking at an elementary level. This text also provides an historical record of one of his demonstration trance inductions, which are different from those he employed later in his teaching seminars in his home.

As an aside, let me point out a problem with interviewing Erickson. He had a way of joining with the person who interviewed him and adapting what he said to the context and person where it was being said. In the many years that John Weakland and I talked with him about therapy and hypnosis, it was necessary to develop what we thought was the best way to bring out his ideas. Of course, at times we offered our own views, but when we wished to have a situation described from Erickson's view, we had to be careful not to first express our own. If we asked whether he did something because of some theory, he was likely to say that was so, with some modifications which he would outline. For example, if he advised a parent to take some action, and we asked if he did that because of conditioning theory, he would talk to us about the incident in terms of conditioning theory. If we merely asked why he did that, or remained silent and waited for him to come up with an explanation, he would offer a quite different and often unique explanation. That is one reason why in my conversations with Dr. Erickson there are long silences. I am waiting for him to come up with his view rather than imposing my own.

In this interview about the film, there is some of that problem. I had studied the film carefully and had certain ideas about why he did something in an induction, but I could not first present those ideas or he might join me in that view. I had to wait until he came up with his reasons and then offer my own version to see what he thought of it. Interviewing Erickson, as with interviewing anyone who thinks in new ways and is trying to find a language for it, requires a special skill and an ability to restrain oneself.

In the room when the film was played were Erickson, myself, Madeleine Richeport, and Robert Erickson, who was running the projector. The discussion began with some prefatory comments by Erickson.

Erickson: The film itself is incomplete. There are sections cut out here and there. Where perhaps I had an arm lift and lower and lift again, and alternate right and left, they might have put in the right, they might have put in part of the right and left alternation. There were certain remarks omitted. Some of them I can recall, in part. Another important thing is that at the time I did that I was exceedingly ill. There were only two people at the meeting that thought I could function. Everybody said I couldn't function. But Ravitz and Yanovski said if Erickson said he can do it, he can do it. I had only this memory of the situation: of crossing that basement room in a wheelchair, working with a number of subjects, and Bertha Rogers' worried face. She was fearful I would fall flat on my face. And the knowledge that there was a lot of distracting noise. And that Dr. A was very resentful that I was on the program. I remember being wheeled part way across that room, and my next memory is being in a taxi cab leaving Philadelphia. Then the next memory is being somewhere on the way to Phoenix, possibly this side of the Mississippi. So what I will remember of the film will be as choppy as the film itself. There are certain things that I can say. And when I say "stop," you stop it.

THE FILM IS PLAYED

(There is a stage. On the left is a table where four volunteer subjects and Mrs. Erickson [who later demonstrated self-hypnosis] are sitting, waiting to take their turns. In this demonstration, the volunteers happen to be all female. On the right, in view of the subjects, Erickson sits facing a young woman subject.)

E Film: **Tell me, have you ever been in an hypnotic trance before?**
Subject #1: **No.**
E Film: **Have you ever seen one?**
Subject #1: **No.**
E Film: **Do you know what it's like to go into an hypnotic trance?**
Subject #1: **No.**

Erickson: Before that girl came up I had looked them over (the five women subjects sitting at the table). And all of them didn't realize that I had looked at each one separately. And then — this isn't an actual memory, it's a knowledge — I selected one who was not at the front end of the line. I selected one who was in perhaps the second or the third seat. So they were totally unexpected. When she first sat down in the chair, I said, "Hi." Now in a scientific meeting where someone is on exhibition, there is a certain amount of self-consciousness. I had said the word "Hi." I not only said it to the girl but to the entire group. "Hi." Then I repeated it more than once. They cut out the "Hi" with some of the last subjects. You don't say "Hi" to somebody in front of a serious audience, you say "Hi" when it's a strictly personal thing. You limit the area to be dealt with. People don't know that, but you personalize the situation by saying "Hi." And that had the effect of isolating the subject from the situation."

Haley: How much of what you say to this first girl, or to the others, is also being said to the other ladies on the platform?

Erickson: All of it is being said, and then there are certain repetitions because the other girls will say, "That can't happen to me." Therefore, you have to have it happen to them. Like lifting the arm. And that gives all of them a realization that hypnosis is possible. Not only for me, but for you and the other fellow.

Haley: Your first statement here was, "Have you ever been in a trance before?" Was that to establish the premise that she was already in one?

(Often Erickson would communicate double meanings, or puns, deliberately. He had once pointed out to me that when he asked, "Have you been in a trance before?" he was suggesting that the person was in a trance now, while appearing to be making a simple query about whether she had experienced it before.)

Erickson: No. I had never met these girls. I made the remarks to that effect, and I had never met them. My first sight of them was when I was in a wheelchair being wheeled to the back of that room, the adjacent room. They had all looked at me; they all knew they were on exhibition on closed television to an audience upstairs. They were aware of the plumbers that were pounding on the pipes around. And the television crew. And they knew there were a lot of people thinking various thoughts. Some of which thoughts, in nursing, would not be desirable thoughts. (The volunteers were probably nurses.) So I had to personalize it. I asked all of them had they ever been in a trance before, because I had specified I wanted to know if any of them had been in a trance. I wanted them to be free to tell me so. But I also wanted to know which ones had previous experience so I could do things more rapidly.

E Film: Did you know that you do all the work, and I just sit by and enjoy watching you work?

Subject #1: No, I didn't know that.

E Film: You didn't know that. Well, I'm really going to enjoy watching you work.

Erickson: "I am going to enjoy watching you work." Which actually means *you* are going to work and I am going to enjoy it. It's a displacement that can't be recognized. And of course you don't mind if I enjoy watching you work.

E Film: **Now the first thing I'm going to do is this. I'm going to take hold of your hand and lift it up. It's going to lift up, like that. (Erickson lifts her hand.) And you can look at it. (He lets go and her hand remains up.)**

Erickson: And watch the movement of my hands. You lift the hand. You first put a reasonable but recognizable pressure on the hand. Then while you're still lifting it, you stop the lifting and you bring about a directing sensation. Start the hand lifting, and then (demonstrating a lifting touch) and that indicates "go higher." But they can't analyze that, and then you can slide your hand off slowly so they aren't quite certain just when your hand left contact with theirs. There is a state of uncertainty. So that they really don't know, "Is my hand being touched or is it free from contact?" And that state of bewilderment allows you to say anything you wish to introduce something else. Because people don't know how to deal with that question. Either you have hold of it or you don't have hold of it, but when you don't know, "Am I holding it or am I not holding it?" And that period of time extends in their reaction.

E Film: **And close your eyes and go deeply, soundly asleep. So deeply, so soundly asleep, so deeply so soundly asleep that you could undergo an operation, that anything legitimate could happen to you.**

Erickson: Ordinarily I would tell her "so deeply so soundly asleep," and then I would look away, and the audience would get the impression that I had abandoned the subject to get back into contact with them, that I was leaving her there alone. That would convey the message, "She alone is doing this." And the subject — as Betty mentioned later (when she demonstrated self-hypnosis) — that she heard me breathing. Has anyone in this room heard anybody breathe? There has been a lot of breathing done, but nobody heard it. But Betty heard it. And the subject heard my breathing, and she knows that my breathing came from a different direction when I turned my head. A breathing sound is altered.

In the technique of hand levitation, "Your hand is lifting higher and higher and higher," your voice is going up. It may be the same tonal quality, but the locus is going up higher and higher, and you're giving the suggestion in a verbal fashion and in the locus fashion. And often when the subject fails to respond to hand levitation, you can start the moving higher and higher and higher, and they'll respond to the rising locus of your voice. The audience doesn't know anything about that. They're just paying attention to the words. Then if the subject still fails to levitate the hand, you can heighten the tone of your words. You can get higher (demonstrating voice rising higher) and higher, which is an exaggeration (his inflection). I can't do that very well, but those with good musical knowledge do it automatically. They don't know it, but if you listen to a very competent person you see that they alter the tone of the voice and they do get higher in the tonal qualities of the voice. So you've got an observable phenomenon. And to others, one is not observed and one which is disregarded, and you've got a multiple manner of suggestion.

And in psychotherapy when you say to your patient, "You can forget about that sort of thing," what have you done? You have been talking to the patient. "You can forget about that sort of thing." (He turns his head.) You are talking about that sort of thing over there. Which has nothing to do with the person. You move it. People respond so nicely to that. The magician distracts your attention; he takes the rabbit out of his robe and puts it in the hat because you are looking at some unessential movement he's making over here. It's a displacement technique, a displacement at a vocal level and at a verbal level. Nobody notices it, but the unconscious does. (As an aside, he discusses the toilet training of children in terms of their learning conscious planning to make it to the bathroom.)

Haley: You put the emphasis on her doing the work. Was there something about her that made you decide to do that?

(Often the hypnotist suggests that the subject is going to do all the work as a way of reassuring an uneasy subject. It is a suggestion that she will be in charge of what happens, and the hypnotist will be a follower. Usually, this is considered a special technique, but there are hypnotists who take it as a philosophy and consider hypnosis to be a situation where the subject is put in charge. Sometimes, techniques become

"schools" when they are misunderstood. In this case my assumption that he was making the subject feel more at ease was not his stated purpose, but he emphasized the larger social context indirectly to make the other subjects feel at ease.)

Erickson: That was to distract the other subjects from the discovery that even while waiting for me they were going to respond to whatever I said to the girl. So I made it very apparent it was she and she alone, so that they could give their attention to that and would not pay attention to what was occurring to them. Because there is a tendency when you know you are going to be a subject. Now you've met Dr. B, haven't you? The first time I met Dr. B she was underweight; she was timid, uncertain, and insecure. She attended a seminar. I looked over the audience. I sighted Dr. B as a subject. I put six chairs on the platform. I got five volunteers. And then I said, "This sixth chair might as well be occupied by someone. How about you?" I addressed Dr. B. I spoke a few words to the first subject and dismissed her from the platform. There were just two on the platform. You could almost see Dr. B realize that *she* was going to be the subject. It was a slow progression. There are five left, four left, I'm going to four, three left, two left. I dismissed four. (inaudible phrase) All of those who were dismissed sat at the side of me. So it was obvious who was the subject. And Dr. B became a very responsive subject. She didn't know that the greater part of my technique in inducing a trance was dismissing the other subjects. And people aren't aware of that sort of thing. The carnival worker is. The carney works that way. A magician works that way. And we all learn it.

Another thing is you become aware of sound. A baby first hears sound. He doesn't know where it comes from. But you learn to recognize eventually sound from below, from above, from the side, in front, in back, in all possible places. Only you don't know that you do that. You can be in a room and you sense something and you look up there. How did you learn to look up there instead of here? And you watch people doing that. This learning of the locus of sound is a very important thing, and I employed that with all the subjects by turning. As I say, I was sick, and I was very careful to keep in contact with the situation. My turns were slow, deliberate, and I made my turns with relocation of my voice very extensive. But it was a hard thing to explain to that audience because they couldn't comprehend the importance of that. But I knew it was important. I knew that I was very sick and that I better be pretty careful in the direction of the patient's attention, visual attention, auditory attention, in some exaggerated fashion. And so much of my behavior was exaggerated.

E Film: **Now I'm going to surprise you, but that's all right. (Erickson takes her ankle and uncrosses her leg.) I will be very very careful about it.**

(It is so unusual for a hypnotist to touch a woman's ankle that it deserves some comment. Hypnosis deals with one of the most important questions in human life: How much power will I let someone have over me? It is in the nature of power that it is threatening since one might be exploited by the person with power. It is also appealing because it is protective and being taken care of is a positive experience. Erickson plays with all aspects of power in his hypnotic work. He gets out from under power by saying the young woman will do all the work of hypnosis while he enjoys watching her work. Then he says he is going to surprise her, but he will be careful about it. Previously he has said that only legitimate things will be done to her. This is a combination of threat (a man touching her ankle) and protection (when he says he will be careful about it). The combination of protection and threat intensifies any relationship. Discussing this action, Erickson has his own unique view.)

Erickson: "I will be very very careful. " Just when did I touch the leg? You can't see it on the film. "I will be very very careful." Careful was followed by me making contact with her leg. Now who was to be careful, she or I? And in that state of doubt all became my favor. You notice she couldn't take the idea, "What's the idea of touching my leg?" She had to start with the word "careful" and the doctor and not with the meaningfulness of the touch.

Haley: Why did you want to move her leg?

Erickson: I wanted to demonstrate to the audience that a total stranger in front of an audience could take hold of a lady's leg and produce a catalepsy. And do it without any preliminary discussion and do it easily, naturally. Because in teaching hypnosis you want to teach the accuracy, the casualness, without letting them know how casual and how uncasual it is. How careful it is.

E Film: **And are you comfortable?**

Erickson: "And are you comfortable?" Yes, very comfortable. Nodding yes. Others don't realize it and don't recognize it. But all our lives we have been conditioned to respond to that sort of thing, only we don't know it.

E Film: **And you can nod your head again. Do you know how the ordinary person nods his head? You really don't, but they nod it this way (nodding his head up and down rapidly). And you nod it this way (slowly nodding).**

Erickson: She nodded her head. Now watch closely. She nodded her head and then there was a perseveration of the movement. In the ordinary waking state you nod your head and then you stop. In the hypnotic state you nod your head at whatever speed is comfortable for you, and then there is a slight perseveration, which tells the experienced operator how well in the trance the subject is.

E Film: **You don't know what I'm talking about but that's all right. And now your hand is going to lift up toward your face. (Erickson lifts her hand.) And you didn't really know that it was that easy, did you? And when it touches your face you'll take a deep breath and go way deep sound asleep.**

Erickson: "You'll take a deep breath and go way sound asleep." If you take the first step, you can make the second step. So you emphasize the first step by "When you touch you will take a deep breath." The emphasis is all put on the second step, and they can safely take the first step without realizing that they are thus being conditioned to take the second step.

E Film: **And you didn't know it would be that easy, did you? And it is so far different from the show-off stage hypnosis, isn't it?**

Erickson: And you proceed minimally there, but you can recognize it.

E Film: **Because you realize that you're the one who is really doing it. You know that, do you not? I am going to ask you to open your eyes. (She opens her eyes.) Hi. Have you been in a trance?**

(Erickson begins a series of awakenings with this subject. Each time he awakens her, it is in such a way as to encourage amnesia. The "Hi" and the question he asks are appropriate behavior if she has just sat down. These encourage her to respond as if that is so, thereby forgetting what has previously happened The way he does it is more evident with later awakenings.)

Erickson: The "Hi" there is reinforcing the distance between us two. That's all. And the subject doesn't become alarmed when they discover they are all alone, and there is only one other person there, because they still have some memory of being surrounded by a large number of people and they are not startled by suddenly finding themselves all alone in a vacuum. The "Hi" reduces it.

Subject #1: I don't know.
E Film: **You don't? You really don't know? I'll tell you the way to find out. Watch your eyelids to see if they start closing on you.**

Erickson: How do you watch eyelids? You've got to move them in order to watch them. The subject doesn't have the time or the sophistication to know that you have to move the eyelids to watch them. It's what could be called an unfair, a sneaky way of getting across a suggestion without making a suggestion. Betty and I were trying to figure out one night what word was appropriate to giving a suggestion without giving a suggestion. Deviousness? How can you really describe that? We couldn't find a single word in the dictionary that seemed to fit.

E Film: **And if they start closing on you that will mean that you've been in a trance. And down they go, that's beautiful, down they go, down they go. That's right. All the way now. And all the way. All the way until they stay shut.**

Erickson: "Until." If you accept the word "until," you are also accepting the word "shut," only that isn't recognized or realized "until." When does "until" end? At the subject's own choice of time. And when should a patient reach a certain weight? Not until its reasonable. The patient can then set a date, when you say, "Let's be reasonable." And if they don't make the weight on the selected date, "Let's be reasonable" has been said. A patient does not despair. The patient can then extend the period of time. In all therapy it's that way.

E Film: And now all that proof came from within you, did it not? And you can talk, and you can understand me. And you can hear. And you can obey instructions. For example, if I ask you to lift your right arm, you can lift your right arm.

(Ordinarily, Erickson informs subjects that they can talk and understand when he considers them in a quite deep trance and wishes not to lose contact with them. Another aspect of this comment is Erickson's curious use of metaphor. Usually, when one says "for example," it is not a directive but a general statement about a hypothetical situation. What Erickson does is make the general statement and then give it as a directive. That is, it is nonthreatening to listen to "for example" since nothing is going to be asked of one, but in that frame Erickson requests an action.)

Erickson: "And you can obey instructions." The question is, what instructions? That's a threat. To counter the threat you raise your arm and also preface it with the same, "You can hear," "You can feel." When it comes to doing "for example," raise your arm. You can do physically anything, only people don't understand that at a conscious level.

Haley: "For example" then is an item in a class, and the rest of the class goes along with it, is what you mean.

Erickson: Yes.

E Film: (Erickson demonstrates by lifting his right arm with his left one, and she lifts her arm.) Slowly lifting up. Now it's stopped.

Haley: Why did it lift that fast?

Erickson: You can back that film up, and if you were to listen to my voice, I think you would notice a greater rapidity in my speech. "And your hand can lift faster." That's exaggerated. And get that effect.

E Film: It's slowly lifting. Now it stopped. And no matter what you try to do it stays right there. And really try hard to put it down. (Her arm jerks slightly downward.)

(The use of the "challenge" is typical in hypnosis, and Erickson uses many varieties from subtle suggestions to forceful requirements. Essentially, the message is, "I want

you to obey me by demonstrating that you cannot disobey me." It can be a frightening
experience not to be able to control one's arm, and Erickson follows this with a
characterization of it as charming and interesting.)

Erickson: And now I'm talking to *you*. I stay right there leaning forward,
which says, "I'm talking to *you*." And emphasizing that interpersonal
relationship.

E Film: The first time in your whole life that you ever experienced
such difficulty lowering your hand. Isn't that right?
Subject #1: Mmm. (smiling)
E Film: Isn't it charming? Isn't it interesting?
Subject #1: Mmhmm.
E Film: That's right.

Erickson: There's a cut there.
Haley: What do you think was cut?
Erickson: I told her to sense a feeling from her hand lowering. I know that
from what I said there. I don't remember it. But it's obvious that I
told her to sense the feeling of her hand lowering, and as she lowered
it and sensed it, it went in a jerky fashion.

E Film: That's right.

Erickson: What's right? It applies to all that she is doing, but you're not
saying everything you are doing is right. You're just saying, "It's right."
But she automatically applies it to everything she does. And you say,
"That's right, Johnny." He feels he's sitting right, standing right,
walking right, writing right, everything. Information or narrowing
it, focusing it. Except that we don't really realize that we do that. Your
contact with Birdwhistell (an authority on body movement) ought
to tell you a lot about that.

E Film: You'll believe that you've been in a trance, if I have you open
your eyes and wake up wide awake? I'd like to have you believe
that you can't be hypnotized. Is that all right?
Subject #1: Yes.
E Film: You know, you can't really be hypnotized, and as soon as you
open your eyes you'll know that.

(Many years ago when I was on Gregory Bateson's project on communication, he formulated the idea of the double bind. It was defined as a paradoxical communication situation where a message at one level conflicted with a message at another level, and the person had to respond and could not leave the field. A classic example was the directive where one person says to another, "Disobey me." The subject can neither disobey nor obey, because disobeying means obeying. Our problem after discovering this paradox was in finding one in human relations. One of the first examples I found was in hypnosis. In the nature of the situation the hypnotist directs the subject to spontaneously respond. How can one respond spontaneously on command? There were also specific directives often used in hypnosis that were obvious binds, and one classic one is present here. Erickson gives the subject a posthypnotic suggestion to say she can't be hypnotized. She faces a paradox: if she follows the posthypnotic suggestion, she is in a trance. Therefore, saying she can't be hypnotized is saying she was hypnotized. If she does not follow the suggestion and says she can't be hypnotized, then she is conceding she was hypnotized. She must admit she was hypnotized no matter what she does.)

Erickson: She can't open her eyes until she *knows* that.
Haley: Come around with that again?
Erickson: She can't open her eyes until she *knows* that. "As soon as you open your eyes you'll know that you can't be hypnotized." She opens her eyes, and that means that she knows she can't be. It's an indirect suggestion without it being recognized.

E Film: **Tell me, do you think you can be hypnotized?**
Subject #1: **No, I don't.**
E Film: **You really don't.**
Subject #1: **No.**
E Film: **I'd like to have you explain this one little thing. (He lifts her right hand, and it stays up in the air.) And did you ever have a strange man lift your hand and leave it in mid-air like that before?**
Subject #1: **No (smiling).**
E Film: **Do you know that in hypnosis, in medical hypnosis, sometimes you want a patient to hold very, very still. So that you can do an operation, do all manner of things with the patient's full cooperation. And you know during an operation you haven't got time to explain to a patient exactly what they should do. For**

example, if I told you to close your eyes, you could close them. *Now*. (Her eyes blink and then stay closed.)

Erickson: You can see her beginning to understand.

E Film: **You can close them so nicely, and keep them closed so nicely. And surgically, that might be a most important thing. The immobility of your right arm might be a most important thing surgically. Now you know medical hypnosis is far different from stage hypnosis. Stage hypnosis is where somebody throws out his chest and widens his eyes...**

Erickson: That explanation was for the benefit of the audience as well as for the other subjects. And I'm talking to all of the subjects there. So I was reassuring the subjects. And I'm reassuring the audience.

(Erickson mentions stage hypnosis in this demonstration more often than he usually does. He spent his life opposing hypnotic charlatanism and differentiating it from medical hypnosis.)

E Film: **(continuing) ...and tells the audience what a great man he is. But what I would like to have you understand is that you as a person are really a very great person, able to do a lot of things that will help you medically. Does that make you feel happy?**

(Erickson typically rewarded subjects for volunteering at his demonstrations, as will be discussed later.)

Subject #1: **Yes.**

E Film: **Now I don't know what your future is going to be, but I hope that if you ever get married and have a baby, that you can have it very comfortably and easily...**

Erickson: "I hope if you ever get married and you have a baby, you will have it comfortably." I'm not just talking to her. I mean everybody. Because that meant I am talking to *all* within my vision.

E Film: **(continuing) ...if you have an operation you can have it** comfortably and easily, that any surgery that you can have will be comfortable and easy. Any dental work that you have will be comfortable and easy. Does that seem agreeable to you?

Erickson: And having talked to the general audience, I can now talk to the subject directly and the audience will naturally remain my audience.

Subject #1: **Very.**
E Film: **Very?**
Subject #1: **Yes.**
E Film: **I'm so glad of that. And I hope you'll keep that knowledge with you for all the rest of your life. And it isn't really ever important for you to know that I hypnotized you; the important thing is for you to know that you did it all by yourself. I'd like to have you take one or two or three deep breaths and wake up wide awake.**

Erickson: And I saw her make the waking up her own process. "One or two deep breaths. And wake up wide awake." She opened her mouth slightly. Parted her eyelids. Continued the elevation of her head. Altered her breathing. That was all done by her. Also, I emphasized there in an exaggerated fashion, all the hypnosis occurs within you. It isn't the doctor or the dentist or psychologist who does it, it is you with a process within yourself. So many doctors when they start hypnotizing, start out thinking they are doing it. And all they are doing is offering suggestions, really hoping the subject will pay attention to at least some of them.

E Film: **Hi. Tell me, what is your first name?**

(Again, Erickson greets the young woman as if she just sat down. Asking her name is appropriate behavior for just meeting. The tendency of the subject is to have amnesia for what had happened in the trance previously.)

Subject #1: **Harriet.**
E Film: **Harriet? I think that's a nice name. Would you like to shake hands with me?**
Subject #1: **Yes.**

E Film: **You would? (Lifts her hand, and it remains up.) You know, shaking hands with me is rather. . .**

Erickson: There you saw me exaggerating the separation of my hand from hers. So the doctors who attended that seminar, that meeting, those that had attended previous seminars had heard me emphasize the importance of minor suggestion, slow actions, and giving the subject time to respond. And giving that time in a way that would not be recognized. So I exaggerated that. And those who had listened to me previously—most of them had—could see it in very exaggerated fashion.

E Film: **And did you know that you could go into a trance that quickly and that easily?**
Subject #1: **No.**
E Film: **You can, can't you, even with your eyes wide open. You know, if you want to, you can see just *you* and *me*. And nothing else. Not even the television cameras, the lights, or anything else.**

Erickson: You know when I say, "You know you can see just you and me," she didn't check up on it. There's no tendency to look and see. She accepted the word unquestionably. And when you don't question a thing, you accept it.
Haley: If you wanted to rule out the television cameras and such, why do you name them to her?
Erickson: For those sophisticated, you name them. Does she make a response to their names ? For example, if I was writing here. She was aware that she was sitting beside the cedar chest and the television. Even though you tried to control it, you made a minimal turn. (laughs) In hypnosis they don't. It's so hard, there's nothing more insulting to a person. Medical students often tried to heckle me. And it was perfectly obvious that I thought that chap was sitting there heckling me, but there was something over there (looking beyond him). And you could see the heckling dwindle down and down. (laughs) And when someone tries to be insulting, you look else-where. And the guy who is trying to insult you says, "Why doesn't he look at me?" He's pretty helpless. And you can cut him down so easily, so quickly. You can practice that on your kids, you know. Isn't

that right, Robert? And you do it in teaching, don't you?

E Film: **Just me. And you don't have to blink your eyes with normal frequency, or anything of that sort. And your hand and arm feel so comfortable. Now close your eyes. (Harriet closes her eyes.) That's right, all the way. And take a deep breath, and wake up. (Harriet opens her eyes.) Let me shake hands again. (They shake hands.) Hi. Harriet, I'm so glad to meet you.**

(Our brains seem to work in such a way that we make social continuities, even if that requires amnesia. In this case, Erickson takes the young woman's hand, leans back separating their hands, and then does various hypnotic directives. Then he takes her hand again, shaking it, and awakens her. He follows this with, "Hi, Harriet, I'm so glad to meet you," as if they had just sat down together. The actions during the handshake will tend to be forgotten by the subject. One can do the same in therapy with hypnosis by starting a sequence, interrupting it for trance experiences, and then continuing the sequence again, thereby giving amnesia for the trance behavior. Erickson taught me this technique, but he chooses a different aspect of it later when I query him about it.)

Erickson: It's best when you're using hypnosis if the subject has the eyes open, you tell them to close their eyes, and then you tell them to awaken. They've had a lifetime of experience of opening their eyes as a part of the awakening. What they don't realize is they're learning that when they close their eyes they go to sleep.

Haley: Were you trying for an amnesia there is why you ended the way you started on that handshake?

Erickson: Yes. If you want to produce an amnesia, a conscious amnesia, you return to the beginning, and terminate at the beginning. And you'll effect an amnesia that way. You can go into a classroom of medical students, and you can say to them, "I want you to remember very carefully. . . (voice trailing off) What's going on there. By the way, what did I start to say? You make an emphatic statement, you interrupt, and you distract their attention. You go back, and surprisingly they have forgotten. "Now I want you to remember!" And when you do that for a class of medical students, for example, as a preliminary to a discussion of hypnosis, to show them that they can be having amnesia induced without hypnosis, then they are much more susceptible to hypnosis. Because they have been convinced by the normal behavior.

E Film: Thank you so much for helping me.

Subject #1: Thank you.

E Film: Do you realize that you really helped me a great deal?

Subject #1: I have?

E Film: I've taken away, I hope, a lot of the mystery of stage hypnotists and all the other charlatans trying to put upon hypnosis. Thank you. And I'm very grateful to you. Are you wide awake now?

Subject #1: Yes.

E Film: That's good. Now do you suppose we ought to have you change seats with somebody else?

Subject #1: Yes.

E Film: All right. (The assistant takes off her microphone.) The girl in the blue dress.

Erickson: I told her to get the lady in the blue dress, because I wasn't going up to the ladies, she was. You ask the subject to bring up somebody. In seminars, how do you deal with resistant subjects? A number will indicate that they are resistant And you call one of them up and let them be resistant. Call the next one by having that subject escort the other person up. And the other person is wondering why he wasn't resistant. By letting the other fellow lead him up, he's transferring his resistance to that person all the way coming up to you. Only they don't realize it.

(With each of these subjects Erickson uses a different approach. For the next subject he does an essentially Rogerian induction by largely repeating back to her what she says. It is interesting that the Rogerian approach, which is claimed to be only reflective and not directive, can be used to induce someone into an hypnotic trance.)

E Film: Tell me, have you ever been in a trance before?

Subject #2: I think so.

E Film: You think so. (Dr. Erickson leans back, then he leans forward and takes her right hand and lifts it.) And who put you in a trance before?

Subject #2: Dr. Yanovski.

E Film: **Dr. Yanovski? That was very nice of him.**
Subject #2: **I enjoyed it.**
E Film: **You enjoyed it. (He leans back while she sits with her hand in the air). And when do you think you'll go into a trance for me?**
Subject #2: **The way my arm feels, I imagine I might be in one now.**

Erickson: "And when do you think you'll go into a trance for me?" She'd been in a trance with Yanovski. "And when do you think you'll go into a trance for me?" You start assessing time, physical feelings, previous experience. Then she noticed her arm. And that told her. You can often do that with an inexperienced subject. In the seminars, after the first morning of lectures, I would mingle with the audience, shake hands with them, ask them where they came from. As I shook hands with them, I would slowly withdraw my hand, alter the focus of my eyes as if I were looking past and beyond them, alter the tone of my voice as if I was talking to someone back there. And those who went into a trance, I could see that right away. Then I could shift the tone of my voice, the focus of my eyes, and say something that I had said when they were fully awake and bring them out of the trance. They had been in a trance and didn't know it, they had an amnesia, and when it came time to pick out a subject in the audience, I had already tested them.

Haley: Was there a reason why you waited until you touched her hand and started to lift it before you asked who had hypnotized her before?

Erickson: My timing was wrong. I had a great deal of pain at that time, and my timing was off.

Haley: What should the timing have been?

Erickson: I should have asked the question before I really touched her hand.

Haley: Why is that?

Erickson: She had seen the other girl develop an hypnotic state. By catalepsy. And my timing was wrong. She didn't really have the opportunity to tell me that she had been Yanovski's hypnotic subject before she was in a trance. So I made the best of it, without betraying my error.

E Film: **The way your arm feels you might be in a trance right now. In what way does your arm feel different?**
Subject #2: **It tingles.**

E Film: **It singles. It's apart from you.**

Haley: What is this "singles"?

Erickson: Have you ever had your leg go to sleep? Hypnotically, you can
get that partial awareness here and there that has the same tingling
effect. My speech was slurred.

Haley: That wasn't deliberate?

Erickson: No.

Haley: It comes out clear as a bell, "singles."

Erickson: I know.

Haley: I thought you were doing some kind of a word device with her.

Erickson: No, that was slurring of my speech.

Haley: Well I'll be darned. Okay.

Subject #2: **No, it tingles, it tingles, it tingles.**

E Film: **No, it just plain singles.**

Subject #2: **No, it tingles, my hand. . .Well now maybe it singles. It
doesn't seem to be so much a part of me as it was before.**

Erickson: There I capitalized on "single." "Singles" is a thing apart. I was
capitalizing on my slurred speech before.

E Film: **Tell me, are your eyes open?**

Subject #2: **Wide open.**

E Film: **You're sure of that?**

Subject #2: **Right now I am.**

E Film: **Right now you are. Are you still being sure of it?**

Subject #2: **Yes.**

E Film: **Are they closing?**

Subject #2: **Not yet.**

E Film: **You're sure?**

Subject #2: **Yes. (Her lids drop.)**

E Film: **All the way. All the way. And stay shut. All the way. All the
way.**

Erickson: As you watch that eyelid behavior. She shows it very nicely. The
fluctuation of her desires. Shall she keep them open or shall she let
them close? So she had closed her eyes. She closes them all the way

and then opens them and then closes them all the way or opens them halfway. "Oh hell, let's let them go all the way shut and stay shut." That's what she did.

E Film: **Stay shut now. (Her eyes remain closed.)**

Erickson: You also notice I didn't offer any suggestions. I offered only questions. They were questions intended to raise a doubt, an uncertainty, and at the same time, my lack of suggestion, my expression of curiosity, of interest me to her, might begin to question, "Are my eyes going to close?" The only way she is going to find out if they are going to close is by closing them. And she doesn't know that's the only way she can find out.

E Film: **Take a deep breath and go way deep into a trance. And in any future hypnosis, whether medical or dental, I hope you'll enjoy it thoroughly, and I hope that never, never will you use hypnosis to entertain people but to instruct them and make them much more aware. Do you mind if I talk about you?**
Subject #2: **No.**
E Film: **It doesn't make you self-conscious, does it?**
Subject #2: **No. Not when you're in trance.**

Erickson: I knew I was thinking that our Society knew I was sick. They were all in doubt about it. I better acknowledge to the audience that I knew it too. So I exaggerated the movement of my arm so they got the message without knowing it. Von looked at it and said, "Why the hell did you have to advertise that you were sick?" He understood.

E Film: **But you can make response to me. Isn't that right?**
Subject #2: **Yes, I can.**
E Film: **And all of your surroundings seem awfully unimportant, do they not?**
Subject #2: **That's right. I'm only conscious of your voice.**
E Film: **You're only conscious of my voice. That's enough, isn't it really?**
Subject #2: **Oh, yes.**
E Film: **You're here for a medical purpose to demonstrate various**

things. And so take a deep breath and rouse up completely rested and refreshed and energetic. (She opens her eyes.) Do you think you're wide awake?

Subject #2: Well. (pause) No, I don't. I can't get my arm down.

E Film: You can't get your arm down.

Subject #2: No.

E Film: You mean your arm is still asleep?

Erickson: Now there I lifted her arm apart from actual induction of trance. I mistimed when I induced a trance before I wanted a trance. So when I awakened her, I awakened her in relationship to a trance induction that occurred in the lifting of her arm. In other words, two different trance states had been established, and she had to awaken in both of them. And I let her demonstrate that she awakened, but she couldn't really be because her hand was still up. She couldn't get it down. And that segmentation of the body is so important in the matter of hypnosis, in medicine, and in dentistry, and color vision experiments, psychological experiments of all kinds. The matter of psychotherapy, you separate things.

Haley: Did you anticipate that? You were that aware?

Erickson: Oh, yes, I was aware.

(The two trances that Erickson refers to are done in a special way if one looks carefully at the film. The question is why the woman's arm stays up when she has been awakened. It might be that he did not awaken her but only appeared to. For example, he might say, "I want you to wake up?" with a slight questioning inflection which the subject will hear, although an audience might not. That question turns a directive into an inquiry. However, in this case he did not suggest awakening in that way. Another explanation is possible when assuming there were two trances involved. They can be described in a series of stages. First, Erickson asks the woman if she has been hypnotized before, and she says, "I think so." Second, Erickson reaches out and takes her hand and lifts it. As he does so, he asks who previously put her in a trance. She says, "Dr. Yanovski." Third, Erickson leans back and says, "And when do you think you will go into a trance for me?" It appears that when Erickson heard the woman had been previously hypnotized, he assumed that if one recalls a previous trance in an hypnotic situation there is a tendency to go back into that trance. Therefore, Erickson took that opportunity to make a trance through association with the previous hypnotist and a separate trance of his own. The lifted arm was part of the trance of the previous

hypnotist. Therefore, when Erickson awakened her from his trance, she was still in the trance of the previous hypnotist. What is impressive is how rapidly Erickson made the decision to make use of the previous trance and separate it from his own.)

E Film: **Let's change things. Let's have the other arm asleep. (He lifts her left arm and the right one drops.) How does that feel?**
Subject #2: **That feels like the other one did now.**
E Film: **That feels like the other one did. Are your eyes wide awake?**
Subject #2: **Yes, I think they are.**
E Film: **You think they are?**
Subject #2: **Right now I am.**
E Film: **You're beginning to have doubts?**
Subject #2: **Well, in this kind of thing you always have doubts. (Her lids lower.)**
E Film: **You always have doubts. And so when the doctor says, "I doubt if you have pain," what's your reaction?**
Subject #2: **(pause) I don't know. I don't suffer from pain very much.**
E Film: **Isn't that nice?**
Subject #2: **I think it's wonderful.**

Erickson: She's educating them by her behavior.
Haley: What?
Erickson: She is educating the viewers by her own behavior. And when the doctor doubts the pain, can you doubt it? It's nice. You can doubt it. And you can see the change in her eyelid movements. And you could recognize that you could be responding to what was being said even though they were not emphatic, you can really be free from pain, which is the wrong way of doing it. You raise a doubt. "Having pain?" The asthmatic child who had psychosomatic asthma. You say to him, "You know you have asthma, and it's hard to breathe. Maybe some of that asthma comes from your discomfort and your fear. You probably wouldn't notice it if only 5 percent came from fear. You probably wouldn't notice it if only 10 percent came just from fear and not from allergic responses. It would be nice to notice that you had only 80 percent due to allergies. You forget about the 20 percent that comes from your fear." And that makes them feel comfortable.

I did that for a 12-year-old boy. His parents were spending 150 dollars a month for medication the family physician prescribed. And for a couple of weeks the boy got along with only about 10 percent of his asthma. And his parents got so alarmed because he wasn't using the medication, he was breathing comfortably. They told him there was something wrong because he really did have a very bad case of asthma. The parents looked at each other, they told me later. "It was our alarm. We frightened our son to death." And I said, "Yes." The parents said, "You told us that that boy can be comfortable and be pleased." We all make mistakes. One thing you don't know is how much damage his asthma has done to his lungs. You really don't know how much emphysema, so why do you take the blame for causing his death? You really don't know if he might not have died. You take the blame right now. You put it very frankly, emphatically, you take the blame now. You really don't know if he might have died from asthma next month. We really don't know how much emphysema he had, whether they killed the kid. In fact, the doctor killed the boy by prescribing that amount of medication. There was nothing they could do about it after the boy was dead. I'm glad they came in to see me afterwards.

E Film: **And even when your dentist works on you, you will feel pain?**

Erickson: That strained effort that I put into my voice. "Even when your dentist works on you." And even when your obstetrician tells you to bear down. It all relates. You can be comfortable.
Haley: Relates to what?
Erickson: It all relates to anything severe, you can feel comfortable.

E Film: **By the way, are you alone here now? Can you see anybody else?**
Subject #2: **No. Not right now I don't.**
E Film: **Just me?**
Subject #2: **Yes.**
E Film: **Is that enough?**
Subject #2: **Right now it is. Yes.**
E Film: **Right now it is, yes. Now close your eyes and take a deep breath and wake up wide awake all over. All over.**
Subject #2: **How can I wake up all over when I can't get my arm down?**
E Film: **How can you wake up all over when you can't get your arm**

down? You know your arm is part of all over. (Her arm falls to her lap.)

Haley: Did you expect that her arm would stay there?

Erickson: But she's had the learning experience of discovering that she could awaken with her arm up. And that comes from the hangover of suggestion. The need to pay attention to every bit of a patient's behavior. Now that wasn't intentional on my part. She furnished a good illustration of the importance of seeing everything possible. And the failure of people to know that "all over" includes their arm as well as their legs. I'll give you a joke. "I'm following your diet, but I didn't lose weight. First I ate breakfast, and then I took the substance that I should have for breakfast." In other words, they take everything they usually take and the diet as well. (Laughter) And that happens so often. That isn't the most ridiculous one that you can find happening. Be sure you wash your right leg carefully. Two weeks later you examine a patient, and you realize you should have said that it is all right to wash the rest of your body. (Laughter) He was washing just the right leg. It's so ridiculous. I've given time to discover that "all over" meant also her arm. But it took time. You see that thinking, understanding, requires time. In just so simple a thing as that.

Subject #2: **Now I think I'm awake.**

E Film: **Now you think you're awake. You know it was very, very nice of you to cooperate with me. You know I don't know how much time I've got, so would you pick the lady in, I think that's a pink dress over there? (The assistant removes the microphone from #2. She leaves, #3 sits down, and the microphone is adjusted.)**

Erickson: Did you notice the speed with which that subject got up? She actually rushed up.

E Film: **You know I'm not the first person to tell you that you've got pretty blue eyes? You know that, don't you?**

Subject #3: **To tell me.**

E Film: **That I'm not the first to tell you that.**

Subject #3: **No.**

Erickson: What is embarrassing? You tell a woman in front of an audience that she has very pretty blue eyes. How does she feel if she knows that she's on exhibition? Cringing. You didn't see any cringing there. That was for the benefit of the more sophisticated. She has already separated herself from the audience. She was attending to me. She didn't know it, but she was already in a trance. And I didn't think I had to do any more to induce a trance. But I did have to meet the needs of the uninformed in the audience.

E Film: You know the astonishing thing is that pretty blue eyes can be awfully, awfully hard to keep open. Take a deep breath and go way deep sound asleep. In orthopedic surgery the most important thing is to have a patient be able to hold an arm or a leg comfortably in an awkward position hour after hour, day after day. I'd like you to feel your hand as anesthetic and comfortable as can be. (He lifts her right hand which remains in midair.) Your arm feels comfortable, does it not?
Subject #3: **Very comfortable.**
E Film: Very comfortable.

Erickson: I don't know whether it was in relation to what was done in England or not, but the question of awkward positions and fatigue and medical needs. An English orthopedist was using hypnosis to do a skin graft on an ankle. And with the patient in the trance state he explained the importance of getting the skin graft from the abdomen and keeping his ankle over the abdomen. A terribly broken ankle. And the patient maintained that state for over two weeks. Very carefully done. It was a necessary graft, but he could have been strapped into position as was ordinarily done. The question arose: could it have been done under hypnosis without benefit of a cast, the straps, and so on, and maintained during the sleeping state? The patient is able to keep in that awfully, awfully awkward position for two weeks.

There are so many things that can be done that people don't know they can be done and won't believe can be done and have to be shown that it can be done. Like what do you call that? Enlarge your right hand and shrink your left hand. How do you do that? You increase the flow of blood to the right hand and delay the flow from it, and you decrease the flow of blood from the left hand and increase the flow away from it. And you watch it on the chart. The right hand gets larger and the left hand gets smaller. It sounds so ridiculous, and yet it's in a physiological laboratory. You close the hands around a container that will maintain a volume and will show changes in increase in volume. And it's surprising how medical students will try to find some way and reluctantly agree that it did happen. You have them do it. The hand is in. You tell them you do exactly as Joe did. And tell them convincingly in the waking state. Then explain you know what the sense of cold is, what the sense of warmth is. And you can let your right hand get cold. You can let the right hand get hot. That will increase the size. Just wait and watch. And then discover that it happened to them even in the waking state. It's so hard to believe people.

And I've produced some anesthesia with Dr. Mead, doctor of physiology. He said, "That's just a pretense, a simulated anesthesia." He spent the next two hours trying to prove there was no anesthesia. Two hours of hard work by himself and the associate professor, who admitted, "Now I'll have to learn something about physiology." It was anesthetic. Then they started to check up on medical texts to find out what information there was on where anesthesia actually occurs. Since then a lot was done at the University of Michigan on the nervous system and anesthesia as in large part a central phenomenon and not a local phenomenon.

E Film: **Very comfortable. And you haven't lost your ability to talk, your ability to speak. By the way, are just you and I here? (E leans forward with his knee touching hers.)**
Subject #3: **Just you and I.**
E Film: **Just you and I are here. It's nice to be alone with you, I think it's delightful to be with you. And I'd like to have you enjoy sleeping deeper and sounder. . .**

Erickson: How advisable was it for me to tell a pretty girl in front of an audience, "I want you to enjoy being alone with me, enjoy sleeping." (Laughs) You wouldn't get by with that very easily, would you? But she didn't seem to notice it. Yet that was a very loaded remark. I had a comment on that later, months later. "How did you know you could get by with such a loaded remark?" Some of my friends said they got awfully uncomfortable when I said that. And that's when many realized that in hypnosis you can establish a sense of comfort if you don't violate the person in any way. I was speaking about comfort, aloneness, not about "you and meness." Aloneness and comfort. You and me is a totally different thing. But aloneness, together, and comfort, and sleeping. All of those are comfortable words. And the setting in which something is said gives it that meaning. Not just the word itself. The story about the mother who reproved her son saying, "Damn it, that hurt." The mother said, "Why did you swear?" "Well, it hurt that much." She said, "God damn it, it didn't hurt that much." There's a difference between "God damn it" and "God damn it." And you find that quite often, frequently in social situations.

Richeport: I'm curious to know if you're in a trance working with any of these subjects.

Erickson: Why do you ask the question?

Richeport: I'm curious to know if at any time when you're working with any patients or in this type of situation, if you find there is a personal advantage to put yourself in trance. If you feel that you learn certain things about the other person.

Erickson: It's very fortunate that you're here. Jay Haley wants to know and learn. You can watch my movements you will notice that most of them are indicative of a state of hypnosis. I'm free to go in and come out and move back and forth. And in your own study you've seen that. I had the opportunity of demonstrating before an audience Sector was in a trance and didn't know it. Herschman was in a trance but didn't know it. Thompson was in a trance and didn't know it, Bob Pearson was in a trance but didn't know it. They could demonstrate it so it could be recognized by others, you could point to behavior, see trance behavior that comes and goes, and you can notice it all through here.

E Film: (continuing) I don't want you ever ever to forget the capacity of your body to do a great variety of things. And your arm feels comfortable, doesn't it?

Subject#3: Very comfortable.

E Film: And you know, if that arm starts lowering, the other one starts lifting, and there isn't a thing you can do about it. (Her right hand lowers and her left hand rises.)

Erickson: They cut a section there.

E Film: **Now one can call that a compulsion, or one can call it some kind of a habit, some kind of a motor response. Would you mind opening your eyes and looking at me? Isn't it astonishing that you and I should be here alone?**
Subject #3: **Yes.**

Haley: Why do you phrase it that way, Milton, "Isn't it astonishing that...?"
Erickson: That's for the benefit of the audience. A failure of the subject to respond to the word astonishing. There is nothing astonishing. There is nothing, absolutely nothing. You can only be astonished to be alone here if you see others here. Now if you're totally unaware of anything, then there is nothing astonishing. You have to have something to cause the astonishment.

E Film: **Have we ever been introduced?**
Subject #3: **Never.**
E Film: **Never? What is your name?**
Subject #3: **Susan.**
E Film: **Susan. My name is Milton. You know my mother gave me that name. A long time ago.**

Haley: Now what are you going into here?
Erickson: Von says it's corny. I pointed out you can be very corny and ridiculous, but you're awfully alone, there's only the two of you, nobody else there, and she can't feel embarrassed, no matter how corny I get. Because there's nobody else. It's a separate kind of situation. Your very question says that you are responding in a totally different way. Von's denunciation of that as too damn corny.

Subject #3: **It's a nice name.**
E Film: **What's that?**
Subject #3: **It's a nice name.**
E Film: **It is? Well, she liked it too. And I've sort of gotten used to it.**

And so it's a nice name so far as I'm concerned. And then it's easy to write.

Erickson: (Laughing) How ridiculous can you be? Without eliciting a feeling, "That's ridiculous."

Haley: What is your purpose in doing that?

Erickson: Of showing that the—let me say that that situation isn't in context with anything else. It's in context only with her and with me. It would be ridiculous if I told Maddy that my name is Milton, it's a nice name, my mother gave it to me, in the context of this room. The context of the presence of others. But we were really alone.

Richeport: Could you have said this to the previous subject?

Erickson: Yes.

Richeport: (continuing) The same kind of. . .

Erickson: You can say ridiculous things in a context only of—well, it is the entire context, there is no other.

Haley: Two or three of us looked at this and decided you were up to something else. And it sounds like a very interesting idea. We decided you were trying to produce regression by first behaving younger yourself, which would provoke her to behave younger, and that would make a regression.

(When a hypnotist regresses a subject to an earlier age, the subject must place the hypnotist in that earlier time by making the hypnotist some other person. If regressed back to childhood, the subject can make the hypnotist another child, or a teacher perhaps. One explanation of what Erickson is doing here, although it is not his explanation, expresses an extreme interpersonal view. Rather than regress the subject and then be changed himself by the subject, Erickson regresses himself and so forces the subject to become younger to make sense of associating with him. If he is childlike, she must be so too, and in that way he regresses her by regressing himself.)

Erickson: In hypnosis there is always regressed behavior. You can see it there because the behavior is out of context. And it is simplified so very much: "It's a nice name."

Haley: "And it's easy to write."

Erickson: "My mother gave it to me." "Your eyes are a pretty blue."

Haley: You were saying what a young boy would possibly say. "My mother gave me that name, it's an easy name to write."

Erickson: And I didn't evoke an adult girl's response, did I? I knew it was safe to do that because first of all . . .

Haley: But you weren't attempting to move her younger or into her past.

Erickson: No, I was illustrating the simplicity of the aloneness. Exaggerating having one's own context entirely within itself. And no relationship to anything else, past, present, or future.

E Film: By the way, have you noticed anything about me? Why do you suppose I carry this (holding up cane)?

Subject #3: **You have a bad leg?**

E Film: Did you ever see me limp?

Subject #3: **No.**

E Film: Do you suppose this is an affectation?

Subject #3: **No.**

E Film: You know, I had a good friend who called it an affectation for two years. And then they discovered that I limped. And they were so surprised. Tell me, can you keep your eyes open?

Erickson: It's the same thing there. The context is just what you see. Just what she heard, just what I said. It has no relationship with the past or the present or the future. It's in total isolation.

Haley: When you arrived, she was up there and watched you use that cane getting from the wheelchair.

Erickson: Yes she did, because I did walk from the wheelchair over to the other chair. But she didn't relate the cane to that. It was about the moment only. And in psychotherapy, if you can bring about a suddenness of the moment, of the hour of the day, of the event, you can deal with it much more effectively.

E Film: You sure?

Subject #3: **Mmhmmm.**

E Film: I'm not. That's right. They are closing. (She blinks and closes her eyes.) That's right. Now take a deep breath and feel rested and refreshed and wide awake all over. Will you do that for me? Hi, Susan.

Subject #3: **Hi.**

E Film: Well, it's been nice knowing you. Why do you have your hand up like that?

Subject #3: **I don't know.**
E Film: **You don't know.**

Erickson: Part of the film was cut out there. I awakened her. She had her eyes open, and I was talking to her, and that heavy hammering was going on (noise of banging pipes). And then there was some heavy hammering going on as she was partially awake and heavy hammering *after* she was awake. They cut out most of that because when she was partially awake, she made a partial response to the hammering. When fully awake, she turned her head and she looked. She just turned it slightly when she was partially awake because the stimulus had been received. Giving a response to the stimulus was obliterated by the trance, so she didn't respond any further.

Another way of illustrating that. You offer a piece of candy to a child, and the child reaches out for it. You can draw your hand back. A child not sophisticated like you reaches out a second time. A Mongolian idiot I offered a piece of candy 150 times, full reaching out 150 times. A diagnosis. No normal person can do that. You can't stand 150 frustrations. When somebody is cussing you out, "What did you say?" You let him have it right in the eye: (laughs) "What did you say?" They begin to get so frustrated they say, "Well, hell, forget it."

E Film: **That lady in gray. I think it's gray. I haven't worked with you before, have I? (Erickson is looking at another subject.) All right, will you get the lady in gray?**

Haley: Milton, this one I thought you dismissed much more brusquely than any of the others.
Erickson: The film was cut.
Haley: It was because of the cutting that it looks like that?

E Film: **(Assistant moves the microphone from #3 to #4.)**

Erickson: She was very brisk in her movements to get up there. She was eager.

E Film: **Now, tell me, how do you like to go into a trance? Quickly**

and suddenly, all at once without any warning just as if you had a broken leg or a broken arm.

Erickson: Without any warning. That's a threatening word. Did you see her widen her eyes at that threatening word? Did you see the alteration in her breathing? A change in her position, the increased alertness. She was already in a trance. Only she didn't know it, and others couldn't recognize it.

Haley: What you are saying there, if I could hear you right, was that when you say something threatening, you then shift to a "for example," or a metaphor.

Erickson: Yes. But here I wanted to illustrate the threatening word "without any warning." And yet it wasn't a threat.

Haley: And then you went right into "for example, if you broke a leg," which was a separate thing then.

Erickson: Yes.

E Film: You lose that pain immediately. All right, do so. RIGHT NOW. And in a deep, sound trance. And you and I are here all alone. And your broken leg doesn't hurt one little bit, does it? And it isn't going to hurt, is it? And can you see the nurses?

Erickson: The film was cut there too. She did have a broken leg. But she didn't make the response looking to see. There is some facial expression as if to say, "Of course I have."

Haley: Well, there's something about this, Milton. You have a way of playing with the edge of a metaphor. You go from "It's like having a broken leg" to "Your broken leg feels better," and you play with what's literal and what's metaphoric in this sort of induction. I gather if there was a piece cut out there, then it isn't too clear to me, but it looked like this girl was quite uncertain if she did have a broken leg or not.

Erickson: I know. There was too much cut out there to follow the transition. Most of that is ruined. We can only take what we see there.

Haley: It's not only in this broken leg but in so many hypnotic suggestions. "Your hand is as heavy as lead," and then it shifts to "It is lead."

Erickson: Yes.

Haley: You seem to be doing that here, which is a different way of doing it, I thought. Because you were making a whole scene out of it. Because actually, if she had a broken leg, there would be a hospital scene. And if this was a medical audience, she could look around and see doctors and nurses.

Erickson: This was in the basement and the audience was upstairs.

Haley: There wasn't an audience sitting in front of this group?

Erickson: No.

Haley: I misunderstood that.

Erickson: It was a television camera and they knew that they were being watched on the TVs upstairs, that there was a whole encirclement of the room so that everybody could see. There was a downstairs audience of plumbers, janitors, hotel workers, nosy butt-ins, stragglers, and what not. Dr. A didn't want it and made it so unpleasant. The hotel made it unpleasant for me. When she saw the orderlies, they cut out the transition to the nurses, and they cut out the interns coming down the hallway. They cut out the—what do you call that, table for transporting patients from one floor to another? She saw other patients. But that was all cut out.

Haley: Okay.

Subject #4: Yes, I see other people.

E Film: You see other people. And you can talk, and you can hear. Tell me, can you keep your eyes open?

Subject #4: Yes.

E Film: You really can? You know I have the greatest doubts about that. I really have. They're closing. (She blinks.) All the way. And staying shut. (Her eyes remain closed.) That's right.

Erickson: You saw, about three sentences before, her eyeballs turn up. Then she had to open her eyes, and when she finally closed them she again turned the eyeballs up. That's why you tell a subject to close your eyes and look at the top of your head, and get the eyes in the sleeping position.

E Film: Really enjoy sleeping deeply and peacefully, and bear in mind that in the future for dental or medical purposes, you can go into a trance very easily and very comfortably. For any legitimate purpose. And you know that, don't you?

Subject #4: Yes.

Erickson: The lifting of her hand was cut out. Everything I said about the lifting of her hand. I don't recall what it was.

E Film: And now your broken leg is healed. And now take a deep breath and feel wide awake and refreshed and energetic. (She opens her eyes.)

Erickson: There was a suggestion about the passage of time that was cut out. I have forgotten if I changed the date from October to March or whatever it was. She did very well. I think I asked if there was so much snow last Christmas. And that was the year that Philadelphia had that horrible blizzard. All right.

E Film: By the way, what is your name?
Subject#4: Mary.
E Film: What?
Subject: Mary.
E Film: Do you always keep your hand up in the air like that?
Subject #4: No, not usually.
E Film: Why are you keeping it up there now?
Subject #4: I don't know. (laughs)
E Film: You don't know. You know, women are the strangest creatures there are. They are delightful. You know, half of my ancestors are women. And I'm so glad of it. What would I do without them? Do you think you can keep your hand up there?

Haley: Now why did that hand stay up after you awakened her?
Erickson: Because I lifted her hand up out of context with something else I was doing. So the lifting of the hand might have been — suppose you take this with your left hand and I lift your right. Your attention is on taking this, so this would be out of context with your right hand. Your right hand will remain up. Your left hand would be free to move naturally.

E Film: Did you ever see a woman successfully disputed before? (Laughter)

Subject #4: No.
E Film: Would you like to see her disputed successfully again? Try keeping your eyes open.

Haley: Milton, why do you make such a thing about females in this one?
Erickson: Well, women range from masculine to very feminine. And this girl was very feminine in her behavior. Therefore, I emphasize it.

E Film: Really try. Try harder. You can do better than that, try harder. Try to keep them from staying closed. (She closes her eyes.) That's right.

Erickson: I told the cameraman repeatedly, "Don't focus on me. It's the subject that's important. Only my words." But you see he played up me much more than he should have, and he omitted really important things, and the film was chopped in that same way.

E Film: You know, women are human beings too. Thank goodness for that. Now take a deep breath and wake up wide awake, feeling rested and refreshed...

Haley: Now why on earth do you say, "Women are human beings too?" It's things like this in this film that are puzzling.
Erickson: There was a chopping of the film cut there. Part of that is omitted.
Haley: Well, what was going on that this would be an appropriate statement for her, "Women are human beings too?"
Erickson: The film is not only chopped up, but it's spliced wrong. It didn't get the correct sequences.
Haley: With this last subject?
Erickson: Yes. The sequences are wrong. And I didn't mention that because not having a memory of the exact thing, I couldn't explain the transitions. I couldn't say anything of value about that, except to say the film was cut and spliced in the wrong way.
Haley: Okay.

(It is typical of Erickson to reward subjects by giving some helpful suggestion to them. Sometimes subjects would indicate a problem, and Erickson would intervene therapeutically without the audience having any idea what he was doing. Erickson

never stopped helping people, whether they asked explicitly for help or they simply showed him a problem. With demonstration hypnotic subjects, Erickson typically gave them suggestions that would be helpful to them, and he always did it in a way that the audience would not know the problem or how he was influencing that person. Sometimes his followers misunderstood his procedure. I recall a disciple demonstrating before a large audience, and he asked that the subject tell him a problem so he could help her with it. The woman was forced to reveal a problem to colleagues and strangers. Erickson would never work that way. He worked in indirect and private ways to reward his subjects for coming up and volunteering. When he influenced a subject in this private way, he was also helping someone who had not explicitly asked him to influence her to change.

Those of us who teach therapists must often restrain them from rushing about helping people who have not asked for help. In Erickson's case I was never concerned about that. Not only was he a benevolent and ethical man, but his judgment on when to influence people and when not to was sound. An additional factor that is sometimes not known is that he thought in a special way about communication in relationship to him. He assumed that if a volunteer subject expressed a problem to him, the subject was not merely reporting a problem but indicating a request for help with that problem. As Gregory Bateson put it, "Every message is both a report and a command." In these situations, Erickson received the indication of a problem as a command, or request, that he do something about it. He responded therapeutically, and maintained confidentiality by working in such a metaphoric way that only the subject knew what was happening. Often the subject only knew because of a later change.

One might assume that Erickson's response to questions about this last hypnotic subject indicate that something is being concealed. Rather than answer a question about why he emphasized female issues in this induction, he shifts to the ways the film was cut. He emphasizes femininity with this subject more than any other. When queried, he said, "Well, women range from masculine to very feminine. And this girl was very feminine in her behavior. Therefore I emphasized it." As a matter of fact, this woman did not seem feminine in her behavior, granting that is a subjective judgment. She wore a masculine suit and seemed less feminine than previous subjects. Even if she was very feminine in her behavior, it would seem odd that Erickson would emphasize that. A possible hypothesis is that Erickson thought, from the ways this woman expressed herself to him, she needed to feel and be more feminine. Therefore, he makes a large issue of how a man finds her so feminine. It is a way he often used his masculinity with female clients. Since he always concealed the problem, he would deny that his emphasis was helping this woman with a problem. After making a close relationship with the subject, by emphasizing femininity, he follows that by stepping back properly as he shows her his fondness for his wife.)

E Film: (continuing) ...energetic, and wake up wide awake. (She opens her eyes.) And now I'm going to have the prettiest girl on the platform. Do you mind my saying that?
Subject #4: **No.**
E Film: Do you know why I say that?
Subject #4: **Your wife?**
E Film: It's my wife. And I've got good judgment.

Erickson: Now how could she have reacted to that statement? And what they omitted there was I used my arm to direct the cameraman to take in the other subjects that the audience could pay attention to. The difference in this girl's response to "It's my wife." Because the other girls being in the movement situation made a response looking toward Betty. And this girl didn't. She and I were in total context. My wife wasn't in it. But for the others Betty was in it, and their heads moved. And I had indicated to the cameraman to include the subjects, but they omitted that.

E Film: And thank you so much for your help.

(In the next part of the film Elizabeth Erickson demonstrates autohypnosis.)

I will not attempt to detail what I believe Erickson was doing in this demonstration, but a few general comments are appropriate. Erickson conducted hundreds of demonstrations like this at seminars and medical meetings. In this one he had only a few minutes with each subject, and yet he behaved as casually as if he had hours. With each subject he demonstrated a different approach. Sometimes he was forceful and overwhelming, and sometimes gentle and encouraging. He would put a subject in charge at one moment, and within that framework paradoxically take charge himself. With all the subjects he demonstrated different kinds of involuntary behavior, usually using the lifting of a hand or an eye closure. He worked with direct suggestions and with indirect influence. Again and again he developed amnesia in various ways, which was his great specialty. His use of puns is not emphasized here but is obvious. He often pointed out how words had multiple meanings and could change meanings depending upon one's vocal emphasis. As an example, he could say, "You won't *know* that," in a way that meant, You won't "*no*" that, meaning it will not be negated. His phrasing is typically calculated, as when he says, "You'll do that, will you not?" As he taught, when told they will do something, some subjects think, "I will not." They cannot resist in that manner if Erickson has already taken the negative away from them. This induction illustrates the complexities of paradox in hypnotic inductions as well as the multilevels of message that constantly occur.

I think it is interesting that Erickson's comments on why he did what he did are so often interpersonal and contextual in this discussion. That is, he often points out that he is communicating to the social context while ostensibly talking with the subject. Some Erickson followers believe he was not interpersonal in his views but focused upon the individual, and that I exaggerated his interpersonal focus. Yet here he often comments that his suggestions were done for the other volunteers, or for the audience, as well as for the subject, perhaps knowing that was my interest. Similarly, his comments were directed toward analyzing the film but also were appropriate for his son who was in the room and for Madeleine Richeport and her interests.

Observing this demonstration, one would never know that Erickson was so ill that day that he had difficulty functioning and could hardly remember what he had done. If he was so skillful when ill, one can only imagine how he conducted such a demonstration when he was well. Having seen a few of those, I can only regret that he was not filmed more often.

9

Typically Erickson

(1993)

As I was planning this paper, I found it difficult to think of something new to write about Milton Erickson. I decided to discuss what is familiar about him—what everyone knows as "typically Erickson." I will present some aspects of his approach and how it differs from others. Some of the cases and ideas will be familiar because I will be repeating published cases. Since, sadly, we will no longer be having new cases by Erickson, we must continue to share and enjoy the finite number we do have.

Many years ago, in the 1950s, Ray Birdwhistell, the authority on body movement, estimated to me that Erickson had 5,000 hard-core fans. He was surprised at the size of that crowd. I was surprised that a psychiatrist would have "fans." Even though he was outside the mainstream of therapy in those days, Erickson was known to a surprising number of people. If someone mentioned him, another person would say, "Did you hear the case of the man who could only pee through a 24-inch wooden tube" (Haley, 1985, p. 154). They would discuss his unique way of solving that problem. When the case was recounted, one realized at once that it was an Erickson case because it was so typical of him. It was also something no other therapist would do.

I once stated that Erickson's cases were as distinctive as a Picasso painting. One knew at once who had created that work of art. The style was bold and unlike that of other artists. To continue the parallel, one must consider the period of time of an artist's work, since styles change over the years. Picasso's early work when he was mastering technique was rather traditional and quite different from his later style. His early work also was influenced by the other artists of his period. What of Erickson's ideas? Did he develop from a more traditional way of thinking about psychiatric classification to a greater appreciation of the social situation in the real world? Or was he always oriented to the real world? What of his therapy approach? Did that change and develop over the years? I think perhaps not. One cannot distinguish an early case of Erickson from a later case with any confidence.

ERICKSON'S MENTORS

Was Erickson influenced in his development by other therapists and teachers of his time? Apparently not.

When we examine the work of Erickson, a question arises. Where did he come from? Who were his predecessors and teachers? What tradition was he working within? He was properly trained in psychiatry, but he did not think like his colleagues who had the same training. When we attempt to place him within some ideological framework, we cannot fit him into the schools of therapy of his time or with the teachers.

Most therapists acknowledge a teacher in their development. Erickson did not refer to a teacher or to the influence of anyone, as I recall. I think he deliberately minimized whoever might have influenced him. He said that he learned about hypnosis as a college student when Clark Hull gave a demonstration at the University of Wisconsin (Haley, personal communication). Could one say, therefore, that Hull was his teacher? Erickson would deny that. He said that after that demonstration he took Hull's subject to his room and hypnotized him himself. In the Fall he took a seminar from Hull. Does that mean Hull was his teacher? No, not necessarily. Erickson said that the seminar focused upon the hypnotic techniques that Erickson had developed during the summer. Therefore, he must have been teaching Hull.

A PERSPECTIVE OF CHANGE

When one is talking about therapy, it is helpful to asssume there are two types of theory in the field that should not be confused. One is the theory of why people behave as they do and how they got that way. The other is a theory of change, or what to do about it. These two theories may not be related. What was distinctive about Erickson was that even when he shared with the field a theory of how people got the way they are, his ideas about how to change them were different from anyone else's. Who else in the 1940s would help a young man, in the way Erickson did, who could pee only through a wooden tube. He had him change the material, size, and length of the tube until he revealed that his penis itself was a tube. Where did that approach come from?

The case can be dated to the days Erickson served on the draft board in the 1940s; thus, it was not a later development. At that time, the only clinical ideas in the field were psychodynamic. Family therapy and behavior therapy had not been born. Any other therapist at that time would have assumed that a person behaved as he did because of repressed unconscious ideas that must be brought into awareness with inter-pretations. How would they have explained the wooden tube, and what therapy would they have done with it? In fact, they would not even have focused on the tube because it was assumed one should not focus on a presenting problem. They would have dwelt on the rich psychopathology behind the tube and its symoblic meaning. Where did Erickson learn to focus his therapy on the presenting problem?

Erickson accepted some psychodynamic ideas and even experi-mented with them. He tested out the psychopathology of everyday life by using hypnosis to suggest an unconscious idea, and then he observed the effect on behavior. At that time, he apparently assumed that some people have symptoms as a result of unconscious ideas built in by their past. What he did to cause change was not like what anyone else did who accepted that hypothesis.

The classic example was the phobia. It was assumed that a phobia was caused by a past trauma that the person had repressed into the unconscious. The orthodox therapy was to bring into awareness that trauma and the feelings around it. Should one describe a therapeutic intervention of that type, one would know it was not typically Erickson. Even though he might accept the premise that a phobia had a past cause, what he did about it was different.

As an example, I would cite the case of an inhibited young woman who was phobic in relation to sex. The assumption was that her mother had frightened her with a lecture warning her against sex; then the mother died. Erickson regressed the young woman back to childhood to a time before the mother had given her the frightening warnings. He talked with her about how mothers give advice that only covers part of a problem, and later they offer a more complete teaching when they know their daughters are mature enough to receive it. He then took the young woman forward in time through Mother's frightening warnings about sex, agreeing with what Mother had said. Then he discussed with the young woman what Mother would have said about sex in the future had she lived. The daughter would then be mature enough to use good judgment in relation to sex and her mother would talk about the positive aspects. The unfortunate death prevented her mother from completing the daughter's education. Now, the young woman was ready to accept what Erickson could provide — the more positive view of sex that Mother would have given had she lived.

Erickson's ideas about what to do to change people set him apart in the field. Other people were providing insight into the past. Erickson was setting out to change the past, as in this case, and more fully in the various February Men cases (Haley, 1986, p. 179). It was also typical of Erickson to accept and agree with the negative comments the mother had made and then to change them. He did not condemn the mother or her sexual views when they were so important to the daughter. Erickson's idea that one should use accepting techniques to change people was controversial at the time, and still is. Other therapists argued that you should not approve of a mother's views on sex with which you do not agree. Erickson would argue that not accepting them would have made him unable to communicate adequately with the daughter. Similarly, it was typical of Erickson to be hard on a client who was accustomed to people being hard on him. He considered it necessary for communication. From whom in our kindly profession did he learn such an idea?

Erickson's view of how to change a phobia appears always to have assumed that the phobic situation must be entered with the person distracted and experiencing a new set of emotions and expectations. He would have a person enter a feared elevator while concentrating only on the sensations in the soles of his feet, or he would have a person prepare for the phobic situation by imaging fears on a screen, thus distancing himself from frightening emotions. He would also go out into the world and take action to resolve a phobia. For example, an elderly doctor came to him to recover from a fear of elevators (Haley, 1986, p. 297). He worked in a hospital on the fifth floor, and he had always up the five flights of stairs. He was afraid to ride in the elevator even though the elevators were run by competent young women and were safe. He was getting old and frail, and he could not continue to make it up the stairs.

There are different ways a therapist might conceptualize this fear and its cause, and different ways to think about how to induce change. What would one consider a typically Ericksonian approach? Let me list what I believe were a few of his assumptions and observations as they might fit this case.

1. He would not ask about past traumas, but would focus upon a change in action in the present. He apparently assumed the phobia would be relieved if the client used an elevator while not experiencing the fear of elevators.

2. Since he focused upon symptoms, he was interested in the details. He learned that the doctor was able to go in and out of an elevator. It was when the elevator moved that he panicked.

3. As always, he observed his client carefully, and noted that the elderly doctor was a very correct, rigid man who was extremely proper in his behavior.

Given these observations and assumptions, could one guess what Erickson's typical intervention would be?

Erickson went to the hospital with the elderly doctor and observed the elevators with him. Since the doctor could go in and out of the elvator, Erickson chose an elevator and asked the young woman operator to hold it on that floor. He had the doctor walk in and out, which he demonstrated he could do. Erickson asked the doctor to walk in and out one more time. This time when the doctor walked in, the operator shut the doors. She said to him, "I can't help myself, I have this desperate desire to kiss you." The prudish doctor said, "Stay away from me, behave yourself." The young woman said, "I just have to kiss you." The doctor said, "Take this elevator up at once!" She pushed the handle and the elevator started to rise. Between floors she stopped it again and said, "We're between floors, no one can see me kiss you." "Take this elevator up," said the doctor, and she did so. The doctor's fear of rising in an elevator ended with that one intervention.

ERICKSON'S USE OF AUXILIARY PERSONNEL

A typical Erickson assumption was that single-session therapy was quite possible. Erickson also typically used auxiliary personnel to achieve his ends, such as hairdressers and dressmakers and elevator operators. How different that was from the therapists of the time who would not even talk to a relative on the telephone, far less involve someone else in the therapy. Where did he get the idea of using auxiliary personnel when no one did that? In fact, he involved his children in his therapy, which no one would have done then, or perhaps even now. In those days, even if a client inquired whether or not a therapist had children, it would not be revealed. The therapist would say, "I wonder why you ask that?" Erickson's waiting room for years was the family living room.

Erickson thought it important for a therapist to be personally involved with a client. He did not think the therapist should be a blank screen or a neutral observer. It was his personal involvement that often induced the change he was after.

ERICKSON AND INSIGHT

When clarifying the idea that Erickson was not in the psychodynamic school, one should note the difference between insight in psychodynamic therapy and Erickson's educational approach. He never made interpretations in the usual sense. If a therapist says, "Have you noticed that the way you respond to your boss is like you responded to your father," one can be sure the therapist was not Erickson. He never used such phrases as, "Isn't it interesting that..." or "Do you realize that..." or "I wonder why you defeat yourself in that way." Yet he often educated clients about themselves. He would not help a slim boy realize he was jealous of his strong brother. But he would help the boy discover that he was slim and quick and so more agile than his large and muscular brother. A primary difference between Erickson's educational approach and the insight of psychodynamicists was that he emphasized the discovery of the positive side. But where did he get this idea? In that early period the clinical field explored only the negative.

Erickson did not provide the usual insight, and he demonstrated that change could occur without people having any understanding of why they had the problem or how they got over it. It was his willingness to change someone without teaching them the cause of the problem that was most typical and most opposed by the therapists who believed that only self-knowledge leads to salvation.

Erickson apparently considered insightful interpretations to be rude. A distinctive characteristic of his therapy was that it was often so courteous. If one hears of a therapist accepting the delusion of a patient and working within it, the odds are the therapist was Erickson. For example, a woman said there was a large bear trap in the center of Erickson's small office (Haley, 1985 p. 232). Since no one else could see it, one might assume this was a delusion, if considered in a psychiatric framework. However, Erickson would not violate that bear trap. In the woman's presence he carefully walked around it each time he left the room. That is typically Erickson.

Other therapists would refuse to participate in such a delusion. They would educate her that the trap was not there and discuss how she was misperceiving the world. Some would consider it a sign she was un-treatable and could only be medicated. Others would consider it unethical not to correct her delusion. Erickson seemed to assume that the introduction of the bear trap was a way of communicating something to him and he would accept that metaphor.

Those of us teetering on the edge of eternity had the privilege of knowing Erickson when he was physically active. He could easily drive around town and visit clients or fly to Schenectady and do a workshop. Those who only knew him confined to a wheelchair could not appreciate that a typical Erickson intervention was a home visit, something not considered by properly trained therapists. He seemed to assume a psychiatrist should be like an old-fashioned family doctor in making himself available.

Erickson often brought about change, in this case and others, without anyone understanding what had happened. Not only did he offer change without awareness, but sometimes also without permission. According to the orthodoxy, change without insight or education was impossible, or it was defined as not really change. Not only would psychodynamicists object to this approach, but so would cognitive therapists, or behavioral ther-apists, or cognitive behavioral therapists, or solution-oriented therapists, or even constructivists.

Let me summarize some of the differences between Erickson and the therapists of his time and raise the question of where he learned to do the opposite of his colleagues. He focused on a presenting problem when they did not. He sought a single-session therapy when he could, and he never argued that long-term therapy was better or deeper. He used auxilliary personnel. He was personally involved. He did not make interpretations or provide insight. Other therapists were helping people remember every miserable moment in their past, and they considered that helping people forget was wrong. Erickson induced amnesia for present and past events. He accepted what clients offered and did not correct their ideas prematurely. He made home visits. Finally, he did not merely offer reflection, but took action and gave directives.

When one attends a large meeting honoring Erickson with a faculty of prominent teachers of the major schools of therapy, one finds that even today most of them are not enthusiasts for this typical Erickson approach. In fact, they are shocked by change without understanding and prefer a more rational approach when dealing with irrational problems. Apparently they had an orthodox source of their ideas. But what was the source of Erickson's ideas?

INFLUENCE WITHOUT AWARENESS

What about the other schools of therapy developing in the 1950s? At that time, new innovations began to appear. One of the few advantages of being older is that one has seen the birth and death of various ideologies and ways of doing therapy. I recall an early instance of the beginnings of a new therapy approach and a serious argument over changing someone outside their awareness. It was in a Veterans Hospital in the 1950s when I was on Gregory Bateson's research project on communication. We were developing a therapy with a family orientation. We shared a building with research psychologists who were developing what was to become behavior therapy.

At one of our lunchtime research presentations, two young psychologists said they wished to present a new idea. The audience was a group of hospital staff, almost all of them psychoanalysts or with a psychodynamic ideology. The leader of that group was the Director of Training. He was an elderly, conservative analyst.

As their presentation, the two young men offered a way to increase the expression of emotions, which was considered important at that time. If you wish a patient to express more emotion, they said, everytime he expresses emotion you nod and smile. When he doesn't, you remain impassive. They said if you do that, you'll have a very emotional patient at the end of an hour. The Director of Training and his analytic colleagues reacted with indignation to this presentation. The Director said this was immoral, if not the behavior of a cad. To influence a person without that person being aware of what you are doing is simply improper. One of the young men said, "Well we do this anyhow. If a patient does what we like, we respond positively, and if he doesn't, we don't respond." The Director of Training said, "If you do it and you don't know you're doing it, that's all right!"

Since we had been studying Erickson, we were not shocked by the use of suggestions outside a client's awareness. It was typically Erickson and had been for years. He would say that directives are more difficult to resist if the subject does not know he is receiving them.

Erickson argued that a therapist should know how to influence a client both in and outside awareness by communicating both directly and indirectly through control of the choice of words and vocal inflections. A therapist should also communicate deliberately with his posture and movements. With that control, he could emphasize certain words in a sentence and so be saying one thing while suggesting another, and perhaps offering a third suggestion with his body movement. How different this was from therapists who considered only words to be communication.

There are two issues here that one typically faces with Erickson. One, he was willing to change people outside their awareness. Two, he did not use positive reinforcements in the usual sense. Were his origins in the learning theories of the behaviorist school? I think they were not. He was using behavioral techniques before they were discovered in the learning therapies, but he did not use the typical positive reinforcements that are at the heart of that school. He did not say, "You did that well. . ." or "That was excellent. . ." or "I like the way you did that. . ." Nor did he use M & M's to reinforce a response. One always knew when Erickson was pleased with what one did. Yet I cannot recall him saying, "You did that well."

ERICKSON AND REINFORCEMENT

Erickson once said to me that one should not compliment patients for acting normal. I think of that when I hear one of my students saying to a client, "Oh, how wonderful, you came on time today." I could generalize from that and say that Erickson did not do the usual positive reinforcement because he assumed the individual should take responsibility for his or her actions. Therefore, if a person did well, Erickson responded as if that contribution belonged to the person, not to him guiding the person. He who reinforces takes the power.

The idea is now built into our culture that behavior can be shaped by positive reinforcements, and so parents and therapists and all guidance people compliment people who are doing what they want. I don't believe Erickson did that. Perhaps others might recall him expressing a positive reinforcement, but I do not. If he did, it was when he had his client in a trance. Then he would emphasize being pleased with certain behavior. Certainly, Erickson shaped behavior and persuaded people to do what he wanted and to even do it more. How did he do that? If he had a child write a sentence a thousand times to improve his handwriting, he would not compliment the child when he brought in the handwriting. He would not say, "Oh, you did wonderfully." Instead, he would say, "That's a clearly written "O" or that "Z" is better than that one. In this way he emphasized the item in the class of positive reinforcements without stating the class.

Even if he did not use positive reinforcement, everyone knew when Erickson was pleased. For example, I struggled for years and finally finished writing the book *Uncommon Therapy*. I sent it to Erickson and received no compliment from him. Yet I learned that he bought many copies to give out to people. His compliment was in action or in other ways than verbal reinforcement.

Erickson also did not typically offer direct criticism as a way of teaching. To cite a personal example, I was treating a woman with phantom limb pain in her right arm that was no longer there. I hypnotized her by having her levitate the phantom limb. She pointed to where it was as it went up. I thought that was rather clever and might deserve a paper. I told Erickson about the case, and he did not particularly respond. He talked of other things. Sometime later, he talked about how one should not hypnotize a person with a focus on what is painful, but rather with a focus on what is pleasant. He said one should not hypnotize a headache case by focusing upon the headache. That evening, or perhaps the next day, I realized that I probably should not have hypnotized that woman by focusing upon her painful arm.

Without positive reinforcements, one cannot be in the school of behavior therapy. Yet somehow Erickson seemed to resist them and go his own way. This is not a minor issue. Erickson was one of the great persuaders. People did what he wished them to do. If he did not achieve that end by positively reinforcing the behavior he liked, then how did he do so? I think there is a research project to be done here that might discover a new way of motivating people—the way of Dr. Erickson.

If Erickson was not within the behaviorist ideology, nor in the psychodynamic ideology, what of systems theory? Could we say that his ideas were based on that therapeutic approach?

Before setting out on that profound subject, let me dwell awhile on the idea of changing people outside their awareness. There is a justifiable controversy over this issue, and Erickson is at the heart of it. However, it is more than just an ethical aspect of Erickson's techniques. The nature of therapy is defined by this issue.

I have always thought we should restrain therapists from helping people who do not wish to be helped. However, I was never concerned about Erickson doing that. I knew him as a kindly person who took responsibility for what he did and whose judgment was sound, or at least agreed with mine. However, other therapists who attempt to follow Erickson are not necessarily that kind, nor are they as sound in their judgment of what people need or indirectly request.

Among the many important aspects of influencing someone outside their awareness, besides the ethical issues, there are two that stand out. One is whether or not you can change people without their being aware of it; two is whether or not influence and change in therapy do not always involve collaboration.

Let us consider an example. A couple had a sexual problem and did not wish to discuss it explicitly. Yet they wanted a change in sexual behavior. If Erickson decided they should change, he might influence them indirectly with metaphor. He would discuss a parallel activity, such as having dinner together, in such a way that he influenced their sexual problem. He would ask if they liked appetizers before dinner to stimulate the juices, or if they just dove into the meat and potatoes. In other cases he might make suggestions and give amnesia so that change was kept out of the client's conscious awareness. He was willing to take the responsibility for changing what he thought should be changed.

When a therapist influences a client with interventions that are subtle and deliberately kept outside the client's awareness, the therapist is on the treacherous ground of changing people without permission, or a contract, to change them.

There are therapists who argue that one should not change people without an agreement to do so. Erickson was willing to work without such an explicit agreement. As an example, it was typical of Erickson to say that if a patient comes in complaining of headaches, and he has tracks on his arm that indicate he is an intravenous drug user, it is the therapist's obligation to try to cure the drug addiction. He should not necessarily make that explicit with the client. If the man wishes to present headaches as the problem, that should be the therapeutic focus; indirect ways should be found to deal with the addiction. Once again, Erickson's therapy might be called courtesy therapy. He did not force people to concede problems, just as he did not force insight on clients by interpreting their body movement to them.

Unlike other therapists in his time, Erickson considered the therapist responsible for the results of therapy. That meant an obligation to use his power to induce change when he could. He was also aware that power is the result of collaboration. It is in the area of collaboration that the nature of influence outside awareness becomes an interesting question. It is an oversimplification to say that one can do therapy by making the client aware of all that you are doing, or that you can do it without the person being aware of your interventions. Those who argue that one should make the client aware of everything one is doing have not thought through this situation. A client can never be fully aware of everything the therapist is doing. In fact, the therapist cannot be fully aware of everything he or she is doing. Even if the therapist tries to reveal all by lecturing the client, if one examines slow-motion films of therapy, it is obvious the interchange is too complex for conscious awareness. Ray Birdwhistell estimated that two people in a conversation exchange 100,000 bits of information per minute. That seems reasonable if one studies films of therapy frame by frame. For example, suppose a client says something, and the therapist uncomfortably looks away, and the client changes to another subject. The therapist does not even know he exerted influence; far less can he share it with the client.

The other aspect of awareness is even more complex. If a therapist communicates a metaphor that the subject responds to outside awareness, can it really be outside awareness? How could the client respond to the suggestion and be influenced if not aware of the suggestion? The suggestion would not have been received.

Let me cite an example in a typical area of interest and investigation by Erickson. He noted that if one hypnotizes a subject and gives him a negative hallucination for a table in the room, the subject will not see the table. The table will be outside his awareness. However, if asked to walk across the room, the subject will walk around the table. Even though the subject is unconscious of the table, he will walk around it. Erickson described this as "unconscious awareness." I suggested to him that this was a contradiction in terms. If one is aware of something, one cannot be unconscious of it, by definition. It seemed to me, and still does, that the language of "conscious and unconscious" is too primitive to deal with these issues.

How is this relevant to therapy? If one gives directives to a subject outside the subject's awareness, and the subject responds correctly to those directives, at some level the subject's mind is receiving the message and cooperating. The person is not unconscious of the directive. It would seem there is a collaboration involved when one is influencing someone outside his awareness. One offers a metaphor, such as discussing a couple having dinner, as an analogy to sexual interchange, and the couple choose within the metaphoric message the ideas relevant to them and their problems. They *choose* to collaborate or not in that sense rather than being robots responding to the therapist's directives. Yet they are not conscious of receiving the metaphoric message. In fact, Erickson taught that if the couple is becoming conscious of the parallels in the metaphor, one should "drift rapidly" away from the subject and return to it later. Incidentally, I always assumed that when a client became aware that Erickson was suggesting something, he might actually be letting the client focus on that so that he or she would not notice another suggestion that was the one he wished the client to receive.

Just as the subject must see the table in order not to see it, the subject receiving a metaphoric directive must be aware of the analogy while responding to it without being aware. For example, when he said the couple should really enjoy dinner together, he was assuming the couple would connect his recommendation with enjoying sex, since they were aware, even though unconsciously, of the suggestion. All of Erickson's storytelling techniques involve communication through metaphor, with or without awareness by the receiver of messages being sent. Erickson typically told stories as an important part of his therapy, unlike other therapists of his time, many of whom hardly spoke at all, or only said, "Tell me more about that." From whom did he learn to tell stories?

Another aspect of collaboration might be emphasized. It was not simply that Erickson gave a directive and the subject followed it. More typically, he gave a directive and the client did it with modifications. The ultimate task that was carried out was often a collaboration.

In summary, there are some generalizations around this issue that are typically Ericksonian. He would accept a person's indirect communication as an indication of a problem, and he was willing to take responsibility for ways a patient should change. For example, at his hypnotic demonstrations, he was often offered a clue as to how the volunteer subject needed help, and he would indirectly supply that without the audience knowing. He was trustful of his own judgment about what should be done. When he made suggestions to influence a person outside awareness, he did it with an assumption that there was an unconscious awareness which he was guiding to follow his directives. He also assumed that clients would modify his suggestions. Some people fear the idea that a therapist might impose his ideas on a client outside the client's awareness and without permission; they should consider the matter to be a more complex collaboration than is usually thought.

The issue is actually broader and includes one's conception of the healing profession. Many therapists choose to educate clients in the therapist's theories. When that is done, clients become a special élite with a knowledge of psychology not shared by the general population. In contrast, one can have as a goal that the client be like ordinary people who have no special knowedge of psychology. It was typical of Erickson to shift people back to normal without educating them in therapy ideology. Erickson typically chose to consider therapy ideas to be the business of the therapist, not of the client, although if a client wanted to know what he was doing, he would explain — as long as it did not interfere with the therapy. I recall him saying that if you examine a normal sample of successful men and women, they have little or no interest in their childhood or in theories about psychology.

SYSTEMS AND FAMILY THERAPY

Erickson liked to say, particularly to my students when they visited, that he was not a family therapist. Yet obviously he did therapy with couples and whole families. How can one explain this? One observation is that he also did not call himself a Gestalt Therapist, or a Psychodynamic Therapist, or a Rogerian Therapist, or an Existential Therapist, or a Brief Therapist. He also did not say he was a Group Therapist. I think he did not like to be classified as a type of therapist. Like most good therapists, he wished to maximize his freedom to maneuver. This means seeing clients in a whole range of different ways.

Erickson liked to approach each case in a unique way rather than follow a method. Most therapists in his time wanted a method to fit everyone into. Erickson did not. To have a label, like "Family Therapist," meant that one could not do a variety of interventions without being accused of unorthodoxy within that label. It also meant one was in a camp with colleagues one might not approve of. I have never chosen to be called a Family Therapist because such a label organizes and limits a therapist's approach. Obviously, any therapist with average intelligence deals with the family, and one does not need to be in a therapy category to do that.

Erickson believed that a therapist received what he or she expected from a client. Systems theory is based on the idea of a self-corrective, governed system that prevents change. If a husband goes too far, the wife reacts; if a wife goes too far, the husband reacts. If they both go too far, the child reacts. Erickson did not like to have therapists expecting people not to change because they were stabilizing a system. He considered resistances of various kinds to be important for a therapist to circumvent, but as I understood him he did not like resistance built into a theory.

One might become academic and raise the question of whether Erickson's therapy had its origins in family therapy. To deal with that, one must define family therapy. That is difficult to do. Erickson typically dealt with families, but not as other family therapists did. However, that is true of other family therapists, since there are different schools of family therapy, each dealing with families differently.

In my research on Erickson's therapy, I encouraged him to talk about his conjoint family interviews because that was what was new in the field at the time. However, more typically, he would see family members separately. At the heart of Erickson's theory was the individual. That was the unit he typically focused upon. A therapist is always the agent of someone, and Erickson typically saw himself as the agent of an individual. He was also willing to expand that unit to include two people. These might be husband and wife, mother and child, or therapist and client. He did not typically expand his problem unit to three people, and so he did not think in terms of coalitions, as some family therapists do. Of course, there were exceptions, but I am talking about his typical ways.

As an example, Erickson once presented to John Weakland and me a case of a woman with extreme sexual inhibitions. Erickson changed her into a rather sexy being, even persuading her to dance into her bedroom nude. Erickson did not deal with her husband. We asked him if he was not concerned about the husband suddenly having to react to a sexually enthusiastic wife. We were thinking within a systems view and assuming the wife and husband had a contract that she was inhibited. This could have been her way of saving her husband from having to deliver sexually. When she changed and made demands upon him, the marriage might well be disrupted. Wasn't it the responsibility of the therapist to deal with that risk? Erickson replied that he was not thinking that way. He said that the husband had passively accepted his wife's inhibitions, and now that she had changed he would passively accept that change. He apparently was not assuming that the wife's problem had a function in relation to the husband, nor that he was triangulating by joining the wife and not the husband. He focused on a woman motivated by individual sexual inhibitions.

However, in other cases of couples, that was not necessarily his premise. For example, a wife came to him with the problem that her husband always had an erection when they went to bed (Haley, 1986, p. 159). It was independent of anything she did. Erickson arranged that the man masturbate excessively and then go into the bedroom without an erection. The wife was pleased to arouse the man. The husband was pleased with the wife's reaction. Is that family therapy? I have not seen a case like that in the family therapy journals.

Let me deal with this issue historically. I met Erickson at one of his seminars in 1953, the same year I joined Gregory Bateson's project on communication. We began investigating hypnosis and John Weakland and I went regularly to Phoenix to talk to Erickson, or he visited us when he came to San Francisco. This began in 1955 and continued over the years. We began to realize that he had a special approach to therapy and we inquired into that as well as into hypnosis. In 1956, I began to do therapy with a family of a schizophrenic on the Bateson project. I also went into private practice that year as a hypnotherapist and marriage therapist. I spent time in 1957 with Erickson talking about cases because I needed supervision for my practice in brief therapy. Erickson was the only one I knew with a brief therapy approach.

The family I was seeing on the project in 1956 was actually an individual therapy, with the parents brought in because the patient was afraid of them. (This was the patient who sent his mother a Mother's Day card saying, "You've always been like a mother to me") (Haley, 1959, p. 357). We did not consider it therapy for the family. However, by April of 1957 we were doing therapy with whole families and calling it family therapy. We were beginning to think in terms of systems theory. I consulted with Erickson over the years, and by 1956 or 1957 I had begun therapy with whole families. Was Erickson already doing therapy with families? It depends upon what one calls therapy with families.

By 1959, the Bateson project held a special conference with Erickson, which we labeled as on marriage and family therapy. At that point, we considered him an authority on that subject. There were only one or two others in the country. By then, we were making use of his family therapy ideas, and perhaps he was using ours as well. Yet he had been dealing with couples and families before we discussed these types of cases with him, so we could not have been the only source of his ideas.

To return to his typical approach in therapy, he often presented a case as an individual problem, and then we would find out that he had also been dealing with family members around the problem.

Let me cite an example from that period. I was in practice in Palo Alto, and an elderly gentleman came to me and asked me if I would treat his daughter for some problems. He told me that he had another daughter who had been treated successfully by a therapist. I asked him why he didn't take this second daughter to the same therapist, since that had gone well. The gentleman said to me that he did not dare do that. When I asked why, he said it was because when he took his daughter to see that therapist, the therapist put him under house arrest for six months. One might guess who the therapist was. I pointed out that he could go back to Erickson and refuse the house arrest. He looked at me as if surprised at my naivete. Finally, I suggested that he return to Dr. Erickson with this second daughter, which he did. It is interesting that Erickson was on good enough terms with the gentleman so that when he visited Palo Alto he stayed in his house. Could one call this case family therapy? I have not seen house arrest therapy in the family therapy catalogue. Yet he was obviously doing therapy with the family to help a daughter or he would not have involved the father in that way.

Erickson's therapy approach raises the issue not only of whether he did family therapy but of what family therapy is. Let me cite some cases to raise the question:

1. When a man was constantly complaining about his fear of dying of a heart attack, although there was nothing wrong with his heart, Erickson had the man's wife distribute funeral literature around the house whenever he complained about his heart (Haley, 1986 p. 178). The man recovered from his fear. Was this individual or family therapy?

2. Early family therapy was often based upon the theory of repression. Therefore, family members were encouraged to talk and express their hostile feelings while the therapist pointed out how negatively they were dealing with each other. The rule was that all family members could say anything, since they were getting out those down deep feelings.

Erickson did not seem to have that view of families or how they should be treated. He was focused upon organizing the family so that specific goals were achieved. When he brought the whole family together, it was in a way that enabled him to control what happened. For example, he had a mother and father and daughter who were yelling complaints at each other. Rather than encourage that, he scheduled them by requiring each of them to complain for 20 minutes. The father, mother, and daughter each had a turn.

In another approach that was typical of him, he prevented free expression in an interview with a whole family. It was a mother, father, and two sons, one of whom was a problem. The mother would not stop talking or allow the others to talk. Erickson asked her if she could hold her thumbs one-quarter of an inch apart. She replied that of course she could. He had her demonstrate. She did so. He said that while she was doing that, he would talk to the others and she should listen so that she could have the last word. He spoke to the son, and the mother answered, but when she did so her thumbs separated more than one-quarter inch. He pointed this out to her and she put the thumbs back again. She could not speak without moving her thumbs, and so she was quiet while he talked with the father and sons, then giving her the last word. Would a family therapist organize an interview that way?

Many family therapists at that time would argue that one should not arrange an interview in such an organized way. Preventing a family member from talking was shocking at a time when free expression was the goal. I recall in the early 1960s Don Jackson, a major family therapist who worked with us, was interviewing a mother and father and their 17-year-old daughter diagnosed as schizophrenic who had just dropped out of college. In the interview, Jackson was talking to the mother when the daughter interrupted. Jackson told the daughter to let her mother speak, and he continued talking with the mother. Jackson did not have as a goal free expression, but was organizing the family to get the girl back to school. A number of therapists at that time were shocked by a therapist restraining someone from speaking, particularly a young daughter with problems.

In that same interview, the mother in the family began to cry, the daughter began to cry, and the father started crying. Jackson politely brought them out of it, but he was clearly irritated. Many family therapists would be pleased if a whole family cried because they would be getting in touch with their feelings. Jackson was interested in getting past the weeping to achieve therapeutic ends. Yet no one said Jackson was not a family therapist.

Erickson did not encourage the expression of feelings as a goal of therapy. He was not really interested in getting people to cry. In fact, he once asked me how I would stop a woman from crying if it was going on too long. Oddly enough, I had no procedure. He said that he would stop her by handing her Kleenex and saying, "At Christmas I give out green Kleenex." That would stop anyone from crying.

3. A couple with a drinking problem came to Erickson and mentioned that their weekends sitting at home were miserable. He sent them out on weekends to go boating on a lake and enjoy the fresh air. That could be considered family therapy. One often hears therapists advising couples and families to do enjoyable things together, to find more pleasure, to take trips together, to seek a vacation from the children, and so on.

Erickson's arrangement of the couple to boat together on the lake was not in this family therapy tradition. He typically advised families to do what they did not want to do. He asked this couple to go boating when he found that neither husband nor wife liked to go boating. They both hated boating on a lake. When they followed his orders and went boating, they found it unpleasant and persuaded Erickson to let them go camping. He allowed that, and they were pleased, since they enjoyed spending pleasant weekends camping. I do not recall that Erickson often sent people out to simply enjoy themselves or vacation together. It is difficult to think of any family therapy school that does not directly encourage more enjoyable behavior in the family. Is Erickson's approach family therapy?

4. A hospital nurse went for a walk behind a building and met a young male staff member there. Sitting down on a bench and talking, they discovered they shared a common situation — he was gay and she was a lesbian. This was a problem for both of them, since there was great prejudice against such a sexual orientation in those days. They would lose their jobs if it was known, and suspicions had already been aroused. After talking together, they become friends and ultimately decided to get married as a cooperative way of concealing their sexual orientation. One might think of this as a fortunate chance encounter of these two people. In fact, Erickson had arranged it. He had suggested to the nurse that she take a stroll behind that building, not saying why, and he arranged that the young man happen to be there. Could this be called family creation?

5. There was a little girl who couldn't do anything and was failing in school. Erickson went to her house each evening and played jacks with her and jumped rope and played other games (Haley, 1986, p. 205). Her parents looked down on such behavior. Is this family therapy? If not, does it become so if one emphasizes how he antagonized the parents by joining the child in this way?

6. In another example that was typically Erickson, a mother and father had a son who wet the bed (Haley, 1986, p. 206). Erickson reports that the mother was a kindly woman trying to help her child. The father was a loud, arrogant man who said he had wet the bed until he was 16 and why shouldn't the boy do that. Erickson said he interviewed the father alone and listened to him at length. The father spoke to him as if he were about 60 feet away. After having heard the father out, Erickson set the father aside and worked with the mother and child to solve the problem. Clearly, he was thinking that both mother and father as well as the child needed to be involved in this case. He was also pleased with the

positive response of the father after the success. That could be called family therapy.

7. Erickson once directed a young man to leave everything and go live alone on a mountain top all alone for one year. Could that be family therapy? Clearly it shows a willingness to disrupt a young man's whole social network.

8. In the 1950s, many women were inhibited about sex, and Erickson was one of the first therapists to do explicit sex therapy to help them overcome their fears. There was no sex therapy at that time, and so he appeared extreme. He also dealt with men who had inhibitions. In one case, a young husband and wife came with the complaint by the wife that the husband was prudish and would not enjoy his wife's breasts (Haley, 1991). Erickson required the young man to give a name to the left breast of his wife, or else Erickson would provide a name he would be stuck with. Was that family therapy?

DIFFERENCES

Let me offer some differences in the ways Erickson and some family therapists viewed problems.

There are two premises that Erickson did not seem to have when dealing with families. He was not thinking of the three-person unit, and so he did not describe a child as caught between mother and father, or expressing a conflict between therapist and parents. He did not think in terms of a triangle, and so did not see that a therapist joining the youth against the parents could increase the youth's problem. He also apparently did not have the theory of motivation that developed in family therapy. One motivation theory is that young people stabilize a family system by having difficulties. They help parents by harming themselves. If a young person shoots heroin, or is delinquent, it can be assumed that it is protective of the family in some way. If a daughter acts up or runs away, it is assumed that it can be a way of helping a depressed mother. If a wife avoids sex, it is hypothesized that she can be protecting her husband from conceding a problem. Erickson did not seem to hold this view of motivation. Not having that view, he did not hypothesize that if a therapist upsets parents, the child can relapse as a way of helping them. One way to upset parents is to side with the child against them.

To put the matter simply, if one assumes a youth is helping parents by failing, there are two approaches. One is to help the parents so the youth does not need to do so. Erickson would, at times, simply tell the young person to leave his parents to him and he would take care of them while the young person went about his business. The other approach is to disengage the youth from the parents and work alone with the child, letting the parents solve their problems on their own. Erickson worked both ways, but I think some of his failures occurred when he joined the child against parents and did not think the parents had to be helped to help the child. He was so fond of children and so irritated with parents who behaved badly that at times he would set out to save children from parents.

Erickson was successful with problem children of all ages, and he particularly enjoyed children. The family view would be that he typically did not take into account the fact that he was triangulating with child and parents, nor did he acknowledge the effect on parents when he succeeded with a child. Parents who have tried and failed to help their child for a long period of time can be upset when a therapist is successful. Erickson would say that they simply needed to adjust to their child becoming normal.

Unlike systems-oriented therapists, Erickson would sometimes tell a young person never to have anything to do with his parents again. He would forbid communication between parents and a youth. Just as he would, at times, tell a wife to leave an abusive husband, he would tell young people to leave abusive parents. He believed that at times parental behavior was so obnoxious and unchangeable that the young person should simply break off contact with the parents.

CONCLUSION

In summary, how did Erickson work differently from others doing a more family-oriented therapy? He did not interview family members together and have them express their feelings as many family therapists did in the early days. Instead, he typically saw family members separately and only occasionally together. He did not always try to have family members communicate with each other if they were not speaking, as therapists with a systems view might do. He was quite willing to separate family members and block them off from contact with each other. He did not typically assume that people harm themselves to help others. He did not map a family in triangles, but more often thought in terms of the individual or the dyad.

As I review here aspects of Erickson that I consider typical, I am aware that what was typical to me might not be typical to others who knew him. Others, for example, might be immersed in his ways of working with hypnosis, which I have not particularly emphasized here. One factor is the period when one knew Erickson. I knew him best in the 1950s when he was active and vigorous and doing seminars all over the country while busy with a private practice. Others have known him in his old age in a wheelchair, where he continued to be powerful but was more limited in what he could do.

To generalize about Erickson is a special problem, since he was different at different times for different people. He tended to speak the language of whomever he was teaching, and he educated with metaphors within which different people could find different meanings. Naturally, when we try to understand him, we try to place him in a category in the field of therapy. Yet, it seems clear he did not operate from any of the standard therapy ideologies of his time. He did not base his ideas on psychodynamic theory or use the basic tool of that approach, the interpretation of the unconscious. He did not accept the basic premises of behavior therapy or use the primary tool, explicit positive reinforcement. He did not accept family systems theory and its basic idea that the behavior of everyone in a system is a product of the behavior of everyone else. Just as he developed his own unique ways of doing hypnosis, he developed his own therapy approach. Now, a decade after his death, we still cannot fit him easily into any of the current or former fashionable schools of therapy.

It is remarkable that a therapist can be so well known and his typical therapy cases so widely reported, while his basic ideology remains in many ways obscure. He was a man who created his own ways. However, I can recall him saying that he was influenced by one particular man. When Erickson was a boy, a kindly doctor cured him of a pain and gave him a nickel. That was when Erickson decided to become a doctor. Perhaps that kindly practitioner not only set him off on his career but provided a model for him. Despite his sophistication, in many ways Erickson worked like a kindly and clever country doctor.

REFERENCES

Haley, J. (1959). The family of the schizophrenic: A model system. *Amer. J. Ment. and Nerv. Dis., 1129,* 357–374.

Haley, J. (Ed.) (1985). *Conversations with Milton H. Erickson, Vol. 1.* Rockville, Md.: Triangle Press.

Haley, J. (1986). *Uncommon therapy.* New York: Norton.

Haley, J. (Ed.) (1991). *Milton H. Erickson. Sex Therapy: The Male.* Audiotape. Rockville, Md.: Triangle Press.